Singapore MATH

LEVEL 6

Appropriate for Students in GRADE **7**

70 Must-Know WORD PROBLEMS

Thinking Kids®
Carson-Dellosa Publishing LLC
Greensboro, North Carolina

Visit carsondellosa.com for correlations to Common Core, state, national, and Canadian provincial standards.

Copyright © 2009 Singapore Asia Publishers PTE LTD

Thinking Kids®
Carson-Dellosa Publishing LLC
PO Box 35665
Greensboro, NC 27425 USA

Printed in the USA • All rights reserved.   ISBN 978-0-7682-4016-0
10-315197784

INTRODUCTION TO SINGAPORE MATH

Welcome to Singapore Math! The math curriculum in Singapore has been recognized worldwide for its excellence in producing students highly skilled in mathematics. Students in Singapore have ranked at the top in the world in mathematics on the *Trends in International Mathematics and Science Study* (TIMSS) in 1993, 1995, 2003, and 2008. Because of this, Singapore Math has gained in interest and popularity in the United States.

Singapore Math curriculum aims to help students develop the necessary math concepts and process skills for everyday life and to provide students with the ability to formulate, apply, and solve problems. Mathematics in the Singapore Primary (Elementary) Curriculum cover fewer topics but in greater depth. Key math concepts are introduced and built-on to reinforce various mathematical ideas and thinking. Students in Singapore are typically one grade level ahead of students in the United States.

The following pages provide examples of the various math problem types and skill sets taught in Singapore.

At an elementary level, some simple mathematical skills can help students understand mathematical principles. These skills are the counting-on, counting-back, and crossing-out methods. Note that these methods are most useful when the numbers are small.

1. The Counting-On Method

Used for addition of two numbers. Count on in 1s with the help of a picture or number line.

$$7 + 4 = \mathbf{11}$$

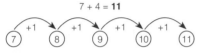

2. The Counting-Back Method

Used for subtraction of two numbers. Count back in 1s with the help of a picture or number line.

$$16 - 3 = \mathbf{13}$$

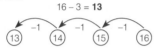

3. The Crossing-Out Method

Used for subtraction of two numbers. Cross out the number of items to be taken away. Count the remaining ones to find the answer.

$$20 - 12 = \mathbf{8}$$

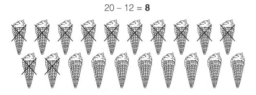

A **number bond** shows the relationship in a simple addition or subtraction problem. The number bond is based on the concept "part-part-whole." This concept is useful in teaching simple addition and subtraction to young children.

To find a whole, students must add the two parts.
To find a part, students must subtract the other part from the whole.

The different types of number bonds are illustrated below.

1. Number Bond (single digits)

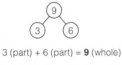

3 (part) + 6 (part) = **9** (whole)

9 (whole) − 3 (part) = **6** (part)

9 (whole) − 6 (part) = **3** (part)

2. Addition Number Bond (single digits)

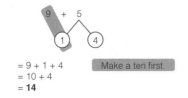

= 9 + 1 + 4   Make a ten first.
= 10 + 4
= **14**

3. Addition Number Bond (double and single digits)

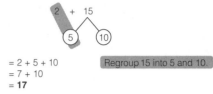

= 2 + 5 + 10   Regroup 15 into 5 and 10.
= 7 + 10
= **17**

4. Subtraction Number Bond (double and single digits)

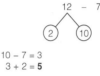

10 − 7 = 3
3 + 2 = **5**

5. Subtraction Number Bond (double digits)

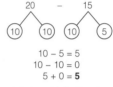

10 − 5 = 5
10 − 10 = 0
5 + 0 = **5**

Students should understand that multiplication is repeated addition and that division is the grouping of all items into equal sets.

1. Repeated Addition (Multiplication)

Mackenzie eats 2 rolls a day. How many rolls does she eat in 5 days?

$$2 + 2 + 2 + 2 + 2 = 10$$
$$5 \times 2 = 10$$

She eats **10** rolls in 5 days.

2. The Grouping Method (Division)

Mrs. Lee makes 14 sandwiches. She gives all the sandwiches equally to 7 friends. How many sandwiches does each friend receive?

$$14 \div 7 = 2$$

Each friend receives **2** sandwiches.

One of the basic but essential math skills students should acquire is to perform the 4 operations of whole numbers and fractions. Each of these methods is illustrated below.

1. The Adding-Without-Regrouping Method

```
  H  T  O
  3  2  1        O: Ones
+ 5  6  8        T: Tens
--------
  8  8  9        H: Hundreds
```

Since no regrouping is required, add the digits in each place value accordingly.

2. The Adding-by-Regrouping Method

```
   H  T  O
  ¹4  9  2       O: Ones
+  1  5  3       T: Tens
---------
   6  4  5       H: Hundreds
```

In this example, regroup 14 tens into 1 hundred 4 tens.

3. The Adding-by-Regrouping-Twice Method

$$
\begin{array}{ccc}
H & T & O \\
{}^{1}2 & {}^{1}8 & 6 \\
+\ 3 & 6 & 5 \\
\hline
6 & 5 & 1
\end{array}
$$

O: Ones
T: Tens
H: Hundreds

Regroup twice in this example.
First, regroup 11 ones into 1 ten 1 one.
Second, regroup 15 tens into 1 hundred 5 tens.

4. The Subtracting-Without-Regrouping Method

$$
\begin{array}{ccc}
H & T & O \\
7 & 3 & 9 \\
-\ 3 & 2 & 5 \\
\hline
4 & 1 & 4
\end{array}
$$

O: Ones
T: Tens
H: Hundreds

Since no regrouping is required, subtract the digits in each place value accordingly.

5. The Subtracting-by-Regrouping Method

$$
\begin{array}{ccc}
H & T & O \\
5 & {}^{7}8 & {}^{11}1 \\
-\ 2 & 4 & 7 \\
\hline
3 & 3 & 4
\end{array}
$$

O: Ones
T: Tens
H: Hundreds

In this example, students cannot subtract 7 ones from 1 one. So, regroup the tens and ones. Regroup 8 tens 1 one into 7 tens 11 ones.

6. The Subtracting-by-Regrouping-Twice Method

$$
\begin{array}{ccc}
H & T & O \\
{}^{7}8 & {}^{9}0 & {}^{10}0 \\
-\ 5 & 9 & 3 \\
\hline
2 & 0 & 7
\end{array}
$$

O: Ones
T: Tens
H: Hundreds

In this example, students cannot subtract 3 ones from 0 ones and 9 tens from 0 tens. So, regroup the hundreds, tens, and ones. Regroup 8 hundreds into 7 hundreds 9 tens 10 ones.

7. The Multiplying-Without-Regrouping Method

$$
\begin{array}{cc}
T & O \\
2 & 4 \\
\times\ & 2 \\
\hline
4 & 8
\end{array}
$$

O: Ones
T: Tens

Since no regrouping is required, multiply the digit in each place value by the multiplier accordingly.

8. The Multiplying-With-Regrouping Method

$$
\begin{array}{ccc}
H & T & O \\
{}^{1}3 & {}^{2}4 & 9 \\
\times\ & & 3 \\
\hline
1,0 & 4 & 7
\end{array}
$$

O: Ones
T: Tens
H: Hundreds

In this example, regroup 27 ones into 2 tens 7 ones, and 14 tens into 1 hundred 4 tens.

9. The Dividing-Without-Regrouping Method

$$
\begin{array}{r}
241 \\
2\overline{)482} \\
-4 \\
\hline
8 \\
-8 \\
\hline
2 \\
-2 \\
\hline
0
\end{array}
$$

Since no regrouping is required, divide the digit in each place value by the divisor accordingly.

10. The Dividing-With-Regrouping Method

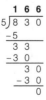

$$
\begin{array}{r}
166 \\
5\overline{)830} \\
-5 \\
\hline
33 \\
-30 \\
\hline
30 \\
-30 \\
\hline
0
\end{array}
$$

In this example, regroup 3 hundreds into 30 tens and add 3 tens to make 33 tens. Regroup 3 tens into 30 ones.

11. The Addition-of-Fractions Method

$$
\frac{1 \times 2}{6 \times 2} + \frac{1 \times 3}{4 \times 3} = \frac{2}{12} + \frac{3}{12} = \frac{5}{12}
$$

Always remember to make the denominators common before adding the fractions.

12. The Subtraction-of-Fractions Method

$$
\frac{1 \times 5}{2 \times 5} - \frac{1 \times 2}{5 \times 2} = \frac{5}{10} - \frac{2}{10} = \frac{3}{10}
$$

Always remembers to make the denominators common before subtracting the fractions.

13. The Multiplication-of-Fractions Method

$$
\frac{{}^{1}3}{5} \times \frac{1}{{}_{3}9} = \frac{1}{15}
$$

When the numerator and the denominator have a common multiple, reduce them to their lowest fractions.

14. The Division-of-Fractions Method

$$
\frac{7}{9} \div \frac{1}{6} = \frac{7}{{}_{3}9} \times \frac{{}^{2}6}{1} = \frac{14}{3} = 4\frac{2}{3}
$$

When dividing fractions, first change the division sign (÷) to the multiplication sign (×). Then, switch the numerator and denominator of the fraction on the right hand side. Multiply the fractions in the usual way.

Model drawing is an effective strategy used to solve math word problems. It is a visual representation of the information in word problems using bar units. By drawing the models, students will know of the variables given in the problem, the variables to find, and even the methods used to solve the problem.

Drawing models is also a versatile strategy. It can be applied to simple word problems involving addition, subtraction, multiplication, and division. It can also be applied to word problems related to fractions, decimals, percentage, and ratio.

The use of models also trains students to think in an algebraic manner, which uses symbols for representation.

The different types of bar models used to solve word problems are illustrated below.

1. The model that involves addition

Melissa has 50 blue beads and 20 red beads. How many beads does she have altogether?

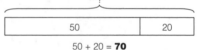

50 + 20 = **70**

2. The model that involves subtraction

Ben and Andy have 90 toy cars. Andy has 60 toy cars. How many toy cars does Ben have?

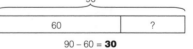

90 – 60 = **30**

3. The model that involves comparison

Mr. Simons has 150 magazines and 110 books in his study. How many more magazines than books does he have?

150 – 110 = **40**

4. The model that involves two items with a difference

A pair of shoes costs $109. A leather bag costs $241 more than the pair of shoes. How much is the leather bag?

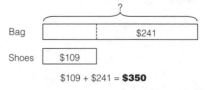

$109 + $241 = **$350**

5. The model that involves multiples

Mrs. Drew buys 12 apples. She buys 3 times as many oranges as apples. She also buys 3 times as many cherries as oranges. How many pieces of fruit does she buy altogether?

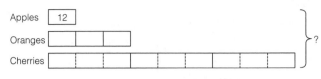

$$13 \times 12 = \textbf{156}$$

6. The model that involves multiples and difference

There are 15 students in Class A. There are 5 more students in Class B than in Class A. There are 3 times as many students in Class C than in Class A. How many students are there altogether in the three classes?

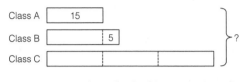

$$(5 \times 15) + 5 = \textbf{80}$$

7. The model that involves creating a whole

Ellen, Giselle, and Brenda bake 111 muffins. Giselle bakes twice as many muffins as Brenda. Ellen bakes 9 fewer muffins than Giselle. How many muffins does Ellen bake?

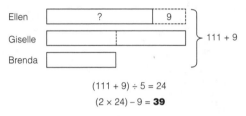

$$(111 + 9) \div 5 = 24$$
$$(2 \times 24) - 9 = \textbf{39}$$

8. The model that involves sharing

There are 183 tennis balls in Basket A and 97 tennis balls in Basket B. How many tennis balls must be transferred from Basket A to Basket B so that both baskets contain the same number of tennis balls?

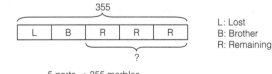

$$183 - 97 = 86$$
$$86 \div 2 = \textbf{43}$$

9. The model that involves fractions

George had 355 marbles. He lost $\frac{1}{5}$ of the marbles and gave $\frac{1}{4}$ of the remaining marbles to his brother. How many marbles did he have left?

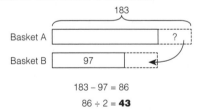

L: Lost
B: Brother
R: Remaining

5 parts → 355 marbles
1 part → 355 ÷ 5 = 71 marbles
3 parts → 3 × 71 = **213** marbles

10. The model that involves ratio

Aaron buys a tie and a belt. The prices of the tie and belt are in the ratio 2 : 5. If both items cost $539,

(a) what is the price of the tie?

(b) what is the price of the belt?

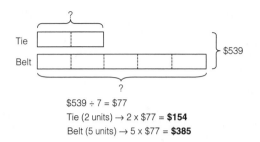

$$\$539 \div 7 = \$77$$
Tie (2 units) → 2 x $77 = **$154**
Belt (5 units) → 5 x $77 = **$385**

11. The model that involves comparison of fractions

Jack's height is $\frac{2}{3}$ of Leslie's height. Leslie's height is $\frac{3}{4}$ of Lindsay's height. If Lindsay is 160 cm tall, find Jack's height and Leslie's height.

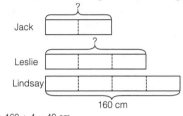

1 unit → 160 ÷ 4 = 40 cm

Leslie's height (3 units) → 3 × 40 = **120 cm**

Jack's height (2 units) → 2 × 40 = **80 cm**

Thinking skills and strategies are important in mathematical problem solving. These skills are applied when students think through the math problems to solve them. Below are some commonly used thinking skills and strategies applied in mathematical problem solving.

1. Comparing

Comparing is a form of thinking skill that students can apply to identify similarities and differences.

When comparing numbers, look carefully at each digit before deciding if a number is greater or less than the other. Students might also use a number line for comparison when there are more numbers.

Example:

3 is greater than 2 but smaller than 7.

2. Sequencing

A sequence shows the order of a series of numbers. *Sequencing* is a form of thinking skill that requires students to place numbers in a particular order. There are many terms in a sequence. The terms refer to the numbers in a sequence.

To place numbers in a correct order, students must first find a rule that generates the sequence. In a simple math sequence, students can either add or subtract to find the unknown terms in the sequence.

Example: Find the 7th term in the sequence below.

1,	4,	7,	10,	13,	16	?
1st term	2nd term	3rd term	4th term	5th term	6th term	7th term

Step 1: This sequence is in an increasing order.

Step 2: $4 - 1 = 3$ $\qquad$ $7 - 4 = 3$
The difference between two consecutive terms is 3.

Step 3: $16 + 3 = 19$
The 7th term is **19**.

3. Visualization

Visualization is a problem solving strategy that can help students visualize a problem through the use of physical objects. Students will play a more active role in solving the problem by manipulating these objects.

The main advantage of using this strategy is the mobility of information in the process of solving the problem. When students make a wrong step in the process, they can retrace the step without erasing or canceling it.

The other advantage is that this strategy helps develop a better understanding of the problem or solution through visual objects or images. In this way, students will be better able to remember how to solve these types of problems.

Some of the commonly used objects for this strategy are toothpicks, straws, cards, strings, water, sand, pencils, paper, and dice.

4. Look for a Pattern

This strategy requires the use of observational and analytical skills. Students have to observe the given data to find a pattern in order to solve the problem. Math word problems that involve the use of this strategy usually have repeated numbers or patterns.

Example: Find the sum of all the numbers from 1 to 100.

Step 1: Simplify the problem.

Find the sum of 1, 2, 3, 4, 5, 6, 7, 8, 9, and 10.

Step 2: Look for a pattern.

1 + 10 = 11	2 + 9 = 11	3 + 8 = 11
4 + 7 = 11	5 + 6 = 11	

Step 3: Describe the pattern.

When finding the sum of 1 to 10, add the first and last numbers to get a result of 11. Then, add the second and second last numbers to get the same result. The pattern continues until all the numbers from 1 to 10 are added. There will be 5 pairs of such results. Since each addition equals 11, the answer is then $5 \times 11 = 55$.

Step 4: Use the pattern to find the answer.

Since there are 5 pairs in the sum of 1 to 10, there should be ($10 \times 5 = 50$ pairs) in the sum of 1 to 100.

Note that the addition for each pair is not equal to 11 now. The addition for each pair is now ($1 + 100 = 101$).

$$50 \times 101 = 5050$$

The sum of all the numbers from 1 to 100 is **5,050**.

5. Working Backward

The strategy of working backward applies only to a specific type of math word problem. These word problems state the end result, and students are required to find the total number. In order to solve these word problems, students have to work backward by thinking through the correct sequence of events. The strategy of working backward allows students to use their logical reasoning and sequencing to find the answers.

Example: Sarah has a piece of ribbon. She cuts the ribbon into 4 equal parts. Each part is then cut into 3 smaller equal parts. If the length of each small part is 35 cm, how long is the piece of ribbon?

$$3 \times 35 = 105 \text{ cm}$$
$$4 \times 105 = 420 \text{ cm}$$

The piece of ribbon is **420 cm**.

6. The Before-After Concept

The *Before-After* concept lists all the relevant data before and after an event. Students can then compare the differences and eventually solve the problems. Usually, the Before-After concept and the mathematical model go hand in hand to solve math word problems. Note that the Before-After concept can be applied only to a certain type of math word problem, which trains students to think sequentially.

Example: Kelly has 4 times as much money as Joey. After Kelly uses some money to buy a tennis racquet, and Joey uses $30 to buy a pair of pants, Kelly has twice as much money as Joey. If Joey has $98 in the beginning,
(a) how much money does Kelly have in the end?
(b) how much money does Kelly spend on the tennis racquet?

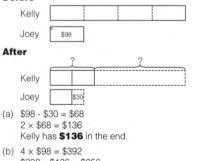

(a) $98 - $30 = $68
$2 \times $68 = $136
Kelly has **$136** in the end.

(b) $4 \times $98 = $392
$392 − $136 = $256
Kelly spends **$256** on the tennis racquet.

7. Making Supposition

Making supposition is commonly known as "making an assumption." Students can use this strategy to solve certain types of math word problems. Making

assumptions will eliminate some possibilities and simplifies the word problems by providing a boundary of values to work within.

Example: Mrs. Jackson bought 100 pieces of candy for all the students in her class. How many pieces of candy would each student receive if there were 25 students in her class?

In the above word problem, assume that each student received the same number of pieces. This eliminates the possibilities that some students would receive more than others due to good behaviour, better results, or any other reason.

8. Representation of Problem

In problem solving, students often use representations in the solutions to show their understanding of the problems. Using representations also allow students to understand the mathematical concepts and relationships as well as to manipulate the information presented in the problems. Examples of representations are diagrams and lists or tables.

Diagrams allow students to consolidate or organize the information given in the problems. By drawing a diagram, students can see the problem clearly and solve it effectively.

A list or table can help students organize information that is useful for analysis. After analyzing, students can then see a pattern, which can be used to solve the problem.

9. Guess and Check

One of the most important and effective problem-solving techniques is *Guess and Check*. It is also known as *Trial and Error*. As the name suggests, students have to guess the answer to a problem and check if that guess is correct. If the guess is wrong, students will make another guess. This will continue until the guess is correct.

It is beneficial to keep a record of all the guesses and checks in a table. In addition, a *Comments* column can be included. This will enable students to analyze their guess (if it is too high or too low) and improve on the next guess. Be careful; this problem-solving technique can be tiresome without systematic or logical guesses.

Example: Jessica had 15 coins. Some of them were 10-cent coins and the rest were 5-cent coins. The total amount added up to $1.25. How many coins of each kind were there?

Use the guess-and-check method.

Number of 10¢ Coins	Value	Number of 5¢ Coins	Value	Total Number of Coins	Total Value
7	7 × 10¢ = 70¢	8	8 × 5¢ = 40¢	7 + 8 = 15	70¢ + 40¢ = 110¢ = $1.10
8	8 × 10¢ = 80¢	7	7 × 5¢ = 35¢	8 + 7 = 15	80¢ + 35¢ = 115¢ = $1.15
10	10 × 10¢ = 100¢	5	5 × 5¢ = 25¢	10 + 5 = 15	100¢ + 25¢ = 125¢ = $1.25

There were **ten** 10-cent coins and **five** 5-cent coins.

10. Restate the Problem

When solving challenging math problems, conventional methods may not be workable. Instead, restating the problem will enable students to see some challenging problems in a different light so that they can better understand them.

The strategy of restating the problem is to "say" the problem in a different and clearer way. However, students have to ensure that the main idea of the problem is not altered.

How do students restate a math problem?

First, read and understand the problem. Gather the given facts and unknowns. Note any condition(s) that have to be satisfied.

Next, restate the problem. Imagine narrating this problem to a friend. Present the given facts, unknown(s), and condition(s). Students may want to write the "revised" problem. Once the "revised" problem is analyzed, students should be able to think of an appropriate strategy to solve it.

11. Simplify the Problem

One of the commonly used strategies in mathematical problem solving is simplification of the problem. When a problem is simplified, it can be "broken down" into two or more smaller parts. Students can then solve the parts systematically to get to the final answer.

Table of Contents

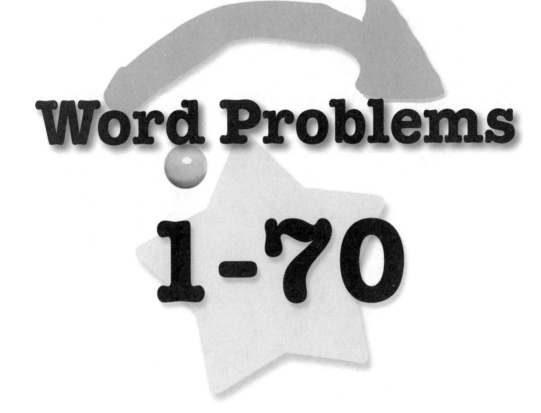

Word Problems

1-70

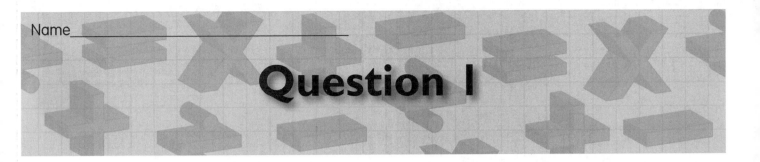
Mr. Lee had a bag of red beans and a bag of black beans. 20% of the total number of beans were black, and there were 180 oz. more red beans than black beans. He transferred some red beans to the bag containing black beans so that the bag now contained 30% of the total number of beans. How many ounces of beans were there in the bag of mixed beans?

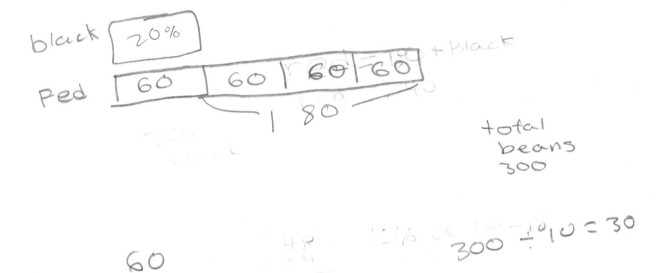

black 20%

Ped 60 | 60 | 60 | 60   red + Black

180

total beans 300

$$300 \div 10 = 30$$

60
+30
___
90

48

90

Answer: _____

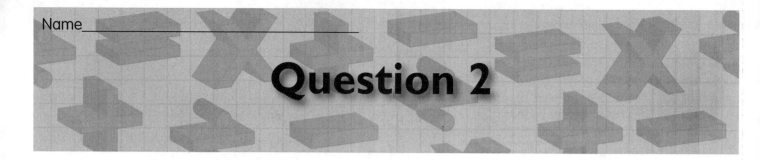
Sarah bought 8 folders and 3 rulers. Lea bought 8 rulers and 3 folders. Sarah paid $1.25 more than Lea. How much was each folder if each ruler was 45¢?

Sarah   8 folders
          3 rulers = 1.35
          8 ruler = 3.60

Lea   3 folders

       45   1.25
      ×   +2.00
       3.60   3.50

       8 3

       3.50
      ÷   5
       .70

Answer: ___70___

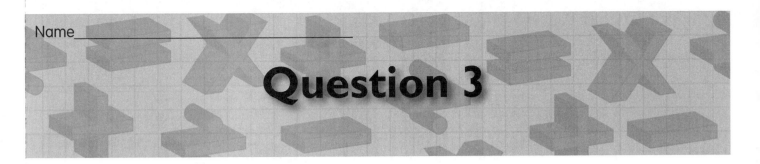
An empty rectangular tank with a base area of 2,400 cm² is filled with water from 2 taps. One tap can fill the tank with 12 L of water per minute, while the other tap can do it at 3 L less per minute.

(a)   What will be the depth of water in the tank after both taps are turned on for 6 minutes ?

(b)   If water leaks from the tank at a rate of 2 L per minute for 6 minutes, what will be the depth of water in the tank ?

2 400 cm

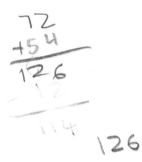

126

Answer: (a) __52.6__

(b) __64__

Name_____

Andy had 20% fewer marbles than Henry. When Andy gave 80 marbles to Henry, the number of marbles he had left was half of what Henry had. How many marbles did Andy have in the beginning?

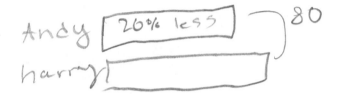

$80 = 30\%$

Answer: ____320____

Question 5

Lily went for 8 rides at the county fair. Some rides were on the merry-go-round, and the rest were on the pirate ship. The total cost of all the rides was $6.30. Each pirate ship ride cost $0.60, and each merry-go-round ride cost $0.90. How many pirate ship rides did Lily take?

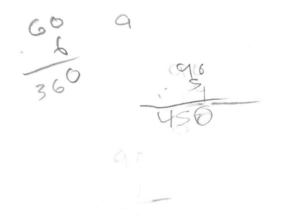

Answer: _____3_____

Question 6

Simon and Jimmy had 167 stamps altogether. Simon gave $\frac{4}{7}$ of his stamps to Trina, and Jimmy gave 37 stamps to Trina. Simon and Jimmy had the same number of stamps left. How many stamps did Jimmy have in the beginning?

Answer: _____

The number of Roberto's baseball cards is $\frac{3}{4}$ the number of David's cards. If Roberto gives $\frac{1}{2}$ of his cards to David, what will be the ratio of Roberto's cards to David's cards?

$$\frac{3}{4} \cdot \frac{1}{2} = \frac{3}{8}$$

$$5:8$$

Answer: ___5:8___

The ratio of boys to girls in a school choir is 4 : 3. There are 6 more boys than girls. If another 2 girls join the choir, what will be the new ratio of boys to girls?

$\frac{3}{4}$

Answer: 13:9 _____

Tierra, Nico, and Alex had $865 altogether. Tierra spent $\frac{2}{5}$ of her money. Nico spent $40, and Alex spent twice as much as Tierra. If the 3 friends had the same amount of money left, how much money did Alex have in the beginning?

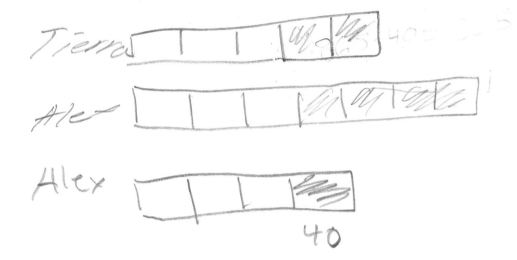

Answer: ___260___

Hitomi has a total of 30 red and blue bowling balls at her bowling alley. Each red ball weighs 8 lb. Each blue ball weighs 9 lb. If the total mass of the blue balls is 49 lb. heavier than the total mass of the red balls, how many red balls does she have?

Answer: _____

In a department store, there were a certain number of red T-shirts, blue T-shirts, and yellow T-shirts. $\frac{2}{7}$ of the T-shirts were red, $\frac{1}{3}$ of them were blue, and the rest were yellow. If there were 20 more red T-shirts than blue T-shirts, how many yellow T-shirts were there?

Answer: _____

Amanda is 12 years old. She is $\frac{2}{7}$ times as old as her father. How many years ago was her father 4 times as old as Amanda?

Answer: _____

Question 13

Daniel gave $\frac{4}{5}$ of his stickers to Javier. Javier's collection of stickers increased to 64. If Javier had 28 stickers in the beginning, how many stickers did Daniel have in the beginning?

Answer: _____

The ratio of the number of postcards John had to the number of postcards Zachary had was 4 : 9. Zachary had 45 more postcards than John. After giving some postcards to John, Zachary had $\frac{6}{7}$ as many postcards as John.

(a)   How many postcards did Zachary have in the beginning?

(b)   How many postcards did Zachary give to John?

Answer: (a) _____

(b) _____

Luisa and Connor had $360 altogether. After Connor gave Luisa $\frac{2}{5}$ of his money, she had the same amount of money as he did. How much money did Connor have in the beginning?

Answer: _____

Name_____

Question 16

There was a total of 840 guests at a wedding dinner. 60% of them were adults, and the rest were children. Some boys left before the dessert was served. As a result, the percentage of adults increased to 70%. How many boys left before the dessert was served?

Answer: _____

Question 17

After Khalil gave Benjamin $\frac{3}{5}$ of the rocks in his collection, Benjamin had 70 rocks. If Benjamin had 25 rocks in the beginning, how many rocks did Khalil have in the beginning?

Answer: _____

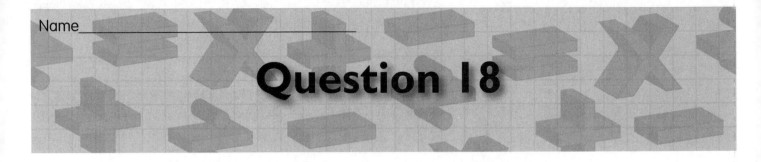

Serena paid $20.20 for 36 rulers and folders. She bought 16 more folders than rulers. If each folder cost $0.50 more than each ruler, how much did each folder cost?

Answer: _____

Question 19

Jackson has 14 pet birds and rabbits. The total number of rabbits have 44 more legs than the total number of birds. How many pet birds does he have?

Answer: _____

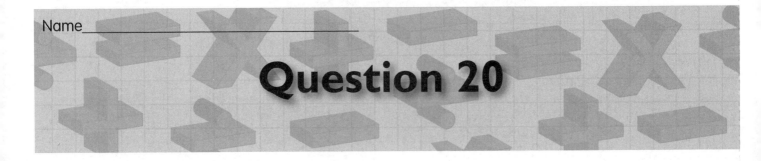

Question 20

Mr. Lynch bought some oranges and pears. After giving away 10 oranges, he had twice as many pears as oranges left. If he had 24 pears in the end, what was the ratio of oranges to pears in the beginning?

Answer: _____

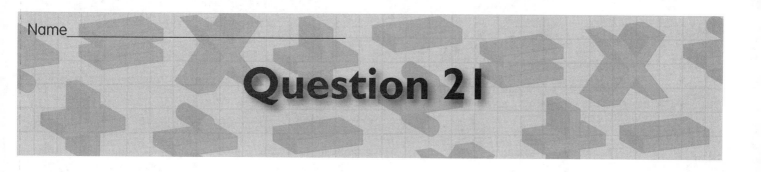

Question 21

The ratio of boys to girls in a classroom was 9 : 8. Half of the girls left the classroom, and then there were 15 more boys than girls.

(a)   How many children were in the classroom in the beginning?

(b)   How many girls left the classroom?

Answer: (a) _____

(b) _____

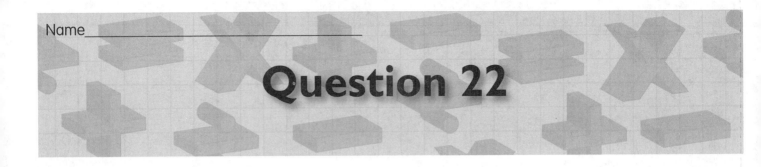

Question 22

Lexi and Maria had $250 altogether. After Lexi spent $\frac{2}{5}$ of her money and Maria spent $40, they had the same amount of money left. How much money did Lexi have in the beginning?

Answer: _____

Question 23

DeShawn and Luke had an equal number of stickers. After DeShawn used 26 stickers and Luke lost 38 stickers, DeShawn had twice as many stickers as Luke. How many stickers did each of them have in the beginning?

Answer: _____

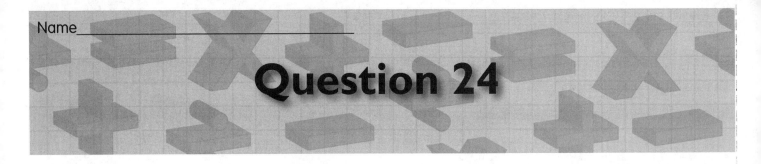

Question 24

There were 75 pebbles in Boxes A, B, and C. After moving 28 pebbles from Box A to B, 24 pebbles from B to C, and 19 pebbles from C to A, there was an equal number of pebbles in each box. How many pebbles were in Box A in the beginning?

Answer: _____

Question 25

Chloe, Emma, and Pilar shared 540 beads. Chloe took 90 beads. Pilar took 3 times as many as the total number of beads Chloe and Emma took. How many beads must Pilar give to Emma so that both receive the same number of beads?

Answer: _____

Question 26

The figure consists of 3 different squares, A, B, and C, which overlap one another. The ratio of their areas is 7 : 8 : 10. $\frac{1}{4}$ of Square B is shaded. What is the ratio of the shaded area to the unshaded areas?

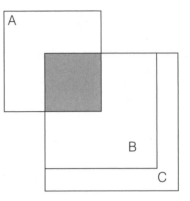

Answer: _____

Name_____

Question 27

Mr. Santiago bought 10 crates of oranges. There were 50 oranges in each crate. He sold 65% of them. 8% of the remainder went bad, and he threw them away.

(a)   How much money did Mr. Santiago earn if he sold the oranges 5 for $1.20?

(b)   If he made $24.15 by selling the rest of the oranges, how much did he charge for each orange?

Answer: (a) _____

(b) _____

Question 28

Jason earns 30 cents for every carrot he sells. He earns an extra $3 for every 30 carrots he sells. How many carrots must he sell in order to earn $555?

Answer: _____

Question 29

Every week, Brady gets $2.50 more for his allowance than Max does. They spend $6 on snacks and save the rest. Brady saves $72, but Max saves only $52.

(a)   How many weeks does it take Brady to save $72?

(b)   How much money does Max get every week?

Answer: (a) _____

(b) _____

Question 30

If Julie bought 8 T-shirts, she would be short $28. If she bought 4 T-shirts and 3 baseball hats, she would have $17 left. If each hat cost $5, how much money did she have in the beginning?

Answer: _____

In March, the total savings of Oliver, Asia, Hassan, and Abby was $1,440. In April, their savings became equal when Oliver's savings doubled, Asia's savings decreased by $30, Abby's savings increased by $46, and Hassan's savings remained the same. Find their total savings in April.

Answer: _____

$\frac{3}{7}$ of the people who live in an apartment building are men. $\frac{5}{8}$ of the remaining people are women. The rest are children. A total of 220 men and women live in the building. How many people live in the apartment building altogether?

Answer: _____

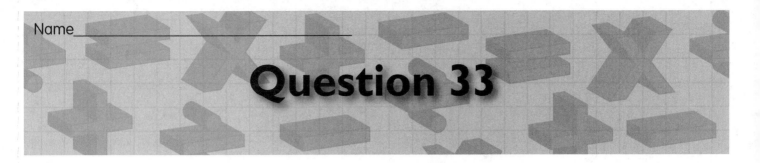

There were 35 gallons of water in a tank and 4.5 gallons of water in a pail. An equal amount of water was poured into the tank and the pail. The ratio of the water in the tank to that in the pail became 7 : 2.

(a)　How much water was in the pail in the end?

(b)　How much water was poured into the pail?

Answer: (a) _____

　　　　　(b) _____

Question 34

Deepak is 10 years old, and his brother is 7 years old. In how many years time will their total age be 41?

Answer: _____

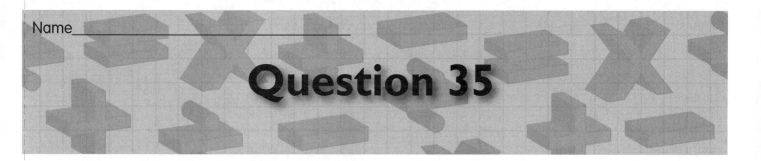

Question 35

The ratio of one-dollar coins to fifty-cent coins in a box was 3 : 4. 6 one-dollar coins were removed, and some fifty-cent coins of the same amount were added. The ratio of one-dollar coins to fifty-cent coins then became 1 : 3. What was the total amount of money in the box?

Answer: _____

A farmer had 500 ducks and 300 chickens. He gave his sister 100 chickens and ducks. Later, the farmer bought 10 more ducks and 75 more chickens. As a result, the number of ducks decreased by 12% and the number of chickens increased by 15%.

(a) How many ducks did the farmer give away?

(b) How many chickens did he give away?

Answer: (a) _____

(b) _____

If Will gives Molly $9, he will have the same amount of money as her. If Molly gives Will $9, the ratio of the money she has to the money Will has will be 1 : 2. How much money does Will have in the beginning?

Answer: _____

Question 38

The ratio of guppies to angelfish in a shop was 2 : 3. The number of angelfish was $\frac{2}{3}$ the number of goldfish. The shopkeeper decided to replace $\frac{1}{4}$ of the guppies with some angelfish. The number of angelfish she added was equal to the number of guppies she replaced. There were 30 more goldfish than angelfish in the end. How many guppies were in the shop in the beginning?

Answer: _____

$\frac{3}{4}$ of the seats in a concert hall were occupied. The ratio of adults to children was 7 : 3. If 90 more adults attended the concert, the number of adults would be 3 times the number of children. How many seats were in the concert hall?

Answer: _____

Question 40

The figure shows 2 similar squares, A and B, which overlap each other. The ratio of the shaded area to the total area of Square B is 3 : 5. The ratio of the shaded area to the total area of Square A is 9 : 17. What is the ratio of the shaded area to the total unshaded areas of the figure?

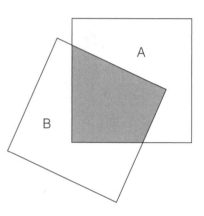

Answer: _____

Question 41

If Owen gives $40 to Charley, they will have an equal amount of money. If Charley gives $80 to Owen, the ratio of Owen's money to Charley's money will be 4 : 1. How much money does Owen have in the beginning?

Answer: _____

Question 42

If 25 dimes were moved from Box A to Box B, there would be an equal number of dimes in both boxes. If 100 dimes were moved from Box B to Box A, the ratio of dimes in Box A to Box B would be 7 : 2. What was the original number of dimes in Box A?

Answer: _____

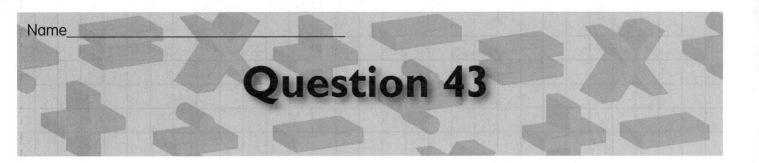

Question 43

80% of the members in a tennis club were male, and the rest were female. After 450 members left the club, the number of male members decreased by 25%, and the number of female members decreased by 50%. Find the number of members in the tennis club in the beginning.

Answer: _____

Question 44

A survey conducted in a school showed that 65% of the students walked to school. The remaining students took buses to school. The ratio of students who took school buses to those who took public buses was 4: 3. There were 360 more students who walked than who took buses. How many students took public buses to school?

Answer: _____

Question 45

There are 32 more apples than oranges in a box. $\frac{3}{5}$ of the oranges and $\frac{1}{3}$ of the apples are overripe. If the number of overripe apples and the number of overripe oranges are the same, how many pieces of overripe fruit are there?

Answer: _____

Question 46

This year, the sum of Mr. Bellini's age and his son's age is 38 years. 4 years ago, Mr. Bellini was 5 times as old as his son.

(a)   How old is his son this year?

(b)   How old is Mr. Bellini this year?

Answer: (a) _____

(b) _____

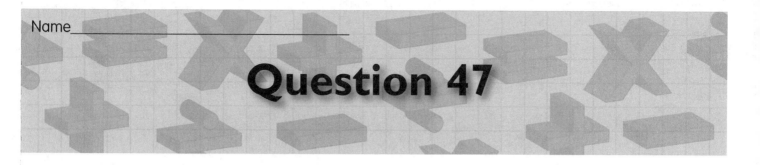

Tap A was turned on to fill a rectangular tank of 50 cm by 40 cm by 28 cm with water at a rate of 6 liters per minute. After 2 minutes, Tap B was turned on to drain water from the tank at a rate of 2 liters per minute. 6 minutes after Tap B was turned on, both taps were turned off. Find the depth of water left in the tank.

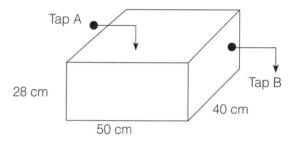

Answer: _____

Question 48

A box contained some red, blue, and green markers. For every 5 red markers, there were 2 blue markers. For every 3 blue markers, there were 5 green markers.

(a)   Find the ratio of red markers to blue markers to green markers.

(b)   When 6 red markers were removed from the box, $\frac{3}{7}$ of the remaining markers were red markers. How many markers were left in the box?

Answer: (a) _____

(b) _____

The figure below is not drawn to scale. The ratio of the area of triangle ABC to the area of triangle DEC to the area of triangle FGH is 7 : 5 : 3. If 20% of the area of triangle DEC is shaded, what percentage of the figure is unshaded?

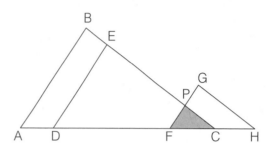

Answer: _____

Question 50

Carter left Town A at noon, driving toward Town B at an average speed of 50 mph. At 12:30 P.M., Minh headed from Town B to Town A along the same road. At 3 P.M., they met each other along the way, and Carter realized that he had completed 60% of his journey.

(a)   How far was Town A from Town B?

(b)   At what speed was Minh traveling?

Answer: (a) _____

(b) _____

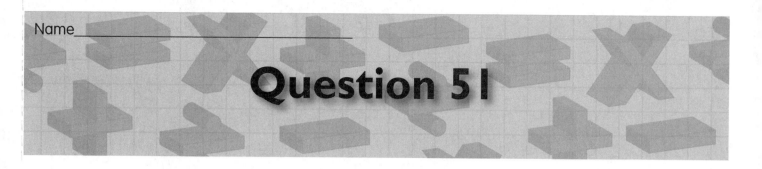

Question 51

Emilio left Sunshine Road at 8:30 A.M. and arrived at Summer Lane at 1:30 P.M. His average speed for the whole journey was 60 km/h. For the first 60% of the trip, he drove at an average speed of 90 km/h. For the next 25% of the remaining trip, his average speed was 60 km/h. Find his average speed for the remaining part of the trip.

Answer: _____

Question 52

At 8 A.M., Dylan and his neighbor, Mickey, drove in their cars to a city that was 240 mi. away from their neighborhood. When Dylan reached the city, Mickey had 40 mi. to go. He finally completed the trip 48 minutes later.

(a)   How long did it take Mickey to drive to the city?

(b)   What was Dylan's driving speed in mph?

Answer: (a) _____

(b) _____

Jada, Nicholas, Nita, and Calvin shared $60. Jada received $\frac{1}{2}$ of the total amount of money Nicholas, Nita, and Calvin received. Nicholas received $\frac{2}{3}$ of the total amount of money Nita and Calvin received. Nita received 3 times as much as Calvin.

(a)   How much money did Jada receive?

(b)   How much more money did Nicholas receive than Calvin?

Answer: (a) _____

(b) _____

Ethan had $8 more than Dakota. Ethan then gave $\frac{1}{4}$ of his money to Dakota. The ratio of money Ethan had to the money Dakota had then became 5 : 7. How much money did Ethan give to Dakota?

Answer: _____

Question 55

Sam had 80 foreign stamps and local stamps. After giving away $\frac{1}{3}$ of his foreign stamps and 10 local stamps, he had an equal number of foreign stamps and local stamps left. How many local stamps did he have in the beginning?

Answer: _____

Mrs. Richmond bought some apples and pears in the ratio 3 : 5. After she gave away $\frac{3}{5}$ of the apples and 40 pears, the ratio of apples to pears became 2 : 5. An apple costs 30 cents. A pear costs 15 cents more than an apple. How much did Mrs. Richmond pay for the fruit?

Answer: _____

Question 57

At the beginning of the year, 40% of the students in the Art Club were boys. In the middle of the year, 25% of the girls left but 8 more boys joined the Art Club. The number of members became 42. Find the total number of Art Club members at the beginning of the year.

Answer: _____

The ratio of Maya's beads to Kayla's beads was 12 : 7. After Maya bought another 28 beads and Kayla gave away 32 beads, $\frac{5}{7}$ of Kayla's beads were left.

(a)   How many more beads did Maya have than Kayla in the beginning?

(b)   Find the new ratio of Maya's beads to Kayla's beads.

Answer: (a) _____

(b) _____

Question 59

At a school camp, 30% of the students were boys. When 87 students left the camp after the second day, half the original number of boys were left behind, and the number of girls decreased by 20%. How many girls were at the camp in the beginning?

Answer: _____

Question 60

Ahmed earns $1.50 for every video game he sells. When he sells one carton of 30 video games, he earns an additional $10. What is the minimum number of video games he has to sell in order to earn $450?

Answer: _____

A certain sum of money was shared among 3 friends, A, B, and C. A received $\frac{3}{7}$ of the money, and B got $\frac{2}{3}$ as much as A. C received $49 less than A.

(a)   Find the ratio of B's money to C's money.

(b)   How much money did C receive?

Answer: (a) _____

(b) _____

Question 62

The ratio of the number of papayas to the number of bananas in a basket is 4 : 5. There are twice as many kiwis as bananas in the basket. If there are 36 more kiwis than papayas, how many pieces of fruit are in the basket?

Answer: _____

$\frac{3}{8}$ of the guests at a birthday party were adults. The ratio of boys to girls was 2 : 7. There were 180 more children than adults. How many more girls than boys were there at the party?

Answer: _____

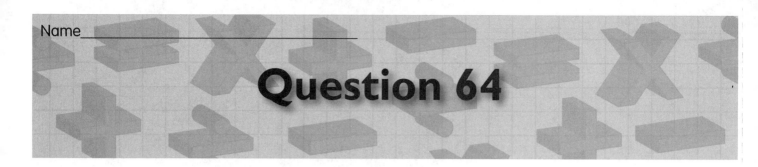
$\frac{3}{5}$ of the people at a funfair were children. $\frac{3}{4}$ of the remaining people were men. There were 140 more children than women. How many people went to the funfair?

Answer: _____

The distance between Town A and Town B was 210 km. At 9:20 P.M., a bus set off from Town A to Town B and a car left from Town B to Town A. The average speed of the bus was 60 km/h, and the average speed of the car was 80 km/h.

(a)   Calculate the time at which the car passed the bus.

(b)   How far had the car traveled when it passed the bus?

Answer: (a) _____

(b) _____

Stephen drove at a constant speed from Town X to Town Y at 9 A.M. yesterday. Half an hour later, Cole drove from Town X to Town Y at a constant speed that was 30 km/h faster than Stephen's. By 9:30 A.M., Stephen had already traveled 40 km. Cole caught up with Stephen at Town Y, arriving at the same time as Stephen.

(a)   At what speed was Stephen driving?

(b)   What was the distance between the 2 towns?

Answer: (a) _____

(b) _____

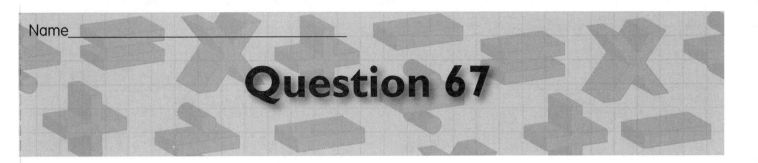
A basket contained 75 brown eggs and some white eggs. Salima found that 15% of the total number of eggs were rotten. Of the rotten eggs, $\frac{2}{3}$ were white and the remaining 6 were brown.

(a)   How many white eggs were there altogether?

(b)   How many eggs were not rotten?

Answer: (a) _____

(b) _____

Ava made 100 paper cranes, and Brittany made $\frac{3}{4}$ of the number of paper cranes Ava made. Ava gave $\frac{9}{20}$ of her paper cranes to Brittany. Then, Brittany gave $\frac{1}{4}$ of her paper cranes to Ava. How many more paper cranes did Brittany have than Ava in the end?

Answer: _____

Question 69

There were 490 children altogether in 2 groups. Group A consisted of only boys, and Group B consisted of only girls. There were $2\frac{1}{2}$ times as many girls as boys. Some girls joined Group B, and for every 4 boys in Group A, 32 more boys joined the group. The total number of girls was then $\frac{1}{3}$ the total number of boys. Express the number of girls who joined Group B as a fraction of the number of boys who joined Group A.

Answer: _____

Last month, Nate spent 12% of his paycheck on car repairs and 25% of the remainder on food. He gave $1,320 of the remaining money to his parents and then bought a computer on sale. If the usual price of the computer was $825 and the discount was 20%, how much money did Nate have in the beginning?

Answer: _____

Solutions to
Word Problems
1-70

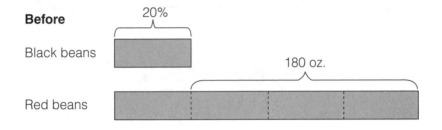

Before

Black beans   20%

Red beans   180 oz.

Since each part is 20%,

$$20\% \times 3 = 60\%$$

3 equal parts are 60%.

$$60\% \rightarrow 180 \text{ oz.}$$

$$10\% \rightarrow 180 \text{ oz.} \div 6 = 30 \text{ oz.}$$

10% of the total number of beans was 30 oz.

$$30\% \rightarrow 30 \text{ oz.} \times 3 = 90 \text{ oz.}$$

There were **90 oz.** of beans in the bag of mixed beans.

Answer: **90 oz. of beans**

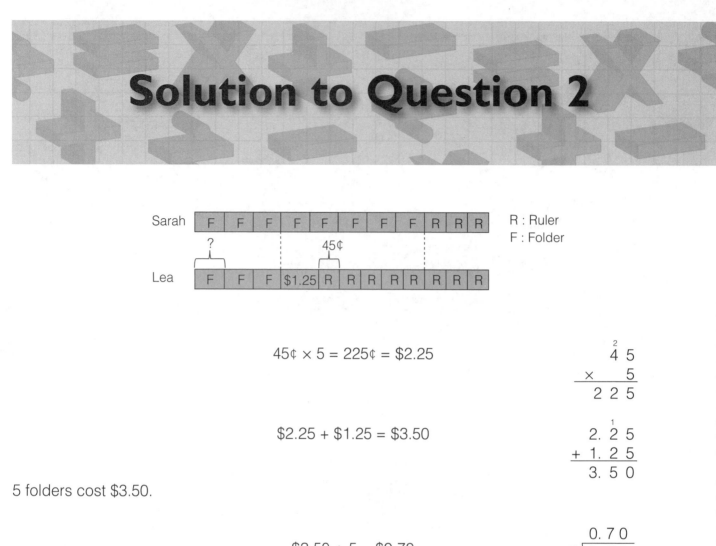

$$45¢ \times 5 = 225¢ = \$2.25$$

$$
\begin{array}{r}
\overset{2}{4}\,5 \\
\times \quad 5 \\
\hline
2\,2\,5
\end{array}
$$

$$\$2.25 + \$1.25 = \$3.50$$

$$
\begin{array}{r}
2.\,\overset{1}{2}\,5 \\
+\,1.\,2\,5 \\
\hline
3.\,5\,0
\end{array}
$$

5 folders cost $3.50.

$$\$3.50 \div 5 = \$0.70$$

$$
\begin{array}{r}
0.\,7\,0 \\
5\overline{)\,3.\,5\,0} \\
-0 \\
\hline
3\,5 \\
-3\,5 \\
\hline
0 \\
-0 \\
\hline
0
\end{array}
$$

Each folder was **$0.70**.

Answer: __**$0.70**__

Solution to Question 3

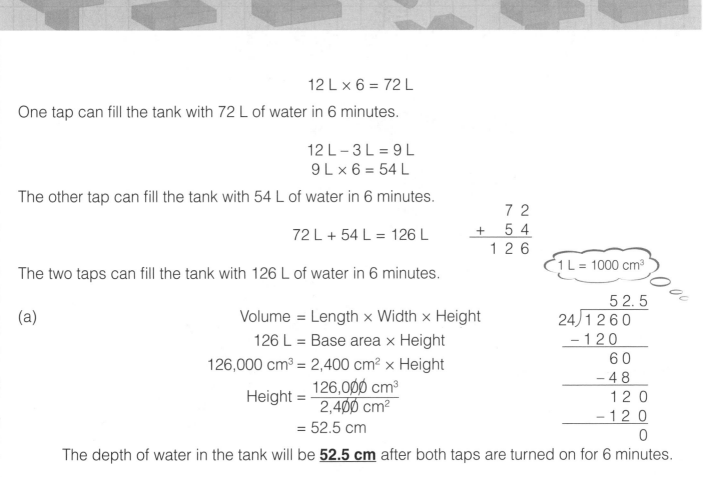

$$12 \text{ L} \times 6 = 72 \text{ L}$$

One tap can fill the tank with 72 L of water in 6 minutes.

$$12 \text{ L} - 3 \text{ L} = 9 \text{ L}$$
$$9 \text{ L} \times 6 = 54 \text{ L}$$

The other tap can fill the tank with 54 L of water in 6 minutes.

$$72 \text{ L} + 54 \text{ L} = 126 \text{ L}$$

```
  7 2
+ 5 4
-----
1 2 6
```

The two taps can fill the tank with 126 L of water in 6 minutes.

1 L = 1000 cm³

(a)
$$\text{Volume} = \text{Length} \times \text{Width} \times \text{Height}$$
$$126 \text{ L} = \text{Base area} \times \text{Height}$$
$$126{,}000 \text{ cm}^3 = 2{,}400 \text{ cm}^2 \times \text{Height}$$
$$\text{Height} = \frac{126{,}0\cancel{0}\cancel{0} \text{ cm}^3}{2{,}4\cancel{0}\cancel{0} \text{ cm}^2}$$
$$= 52.5 \text{ cm}$$

```
       5 2. 5
24) 1 2 6 0
   - 1 2 0
   -------
         6 0
       - 4 8
       -----
       1 2 0
     - 1 2 0
     -------
             0
```

The depth of water in the tank will be **52.5 cm** after both taps are turned on for 6 minutes.

(b)
$$2 \text{ L} \times 6 = 12 \text{ L}$$

12 L of water will leak in 6 minutes.

$$126 \text{ L} - 12 \text{ L} = 114 \text{ L}$$

$$114{,}000 \text{ cm}^3 = 2{,}400 \text{ cm}^2 \times \text{Height}$$

$$\text{Height} = \frac{114{,}0\cancel{0}\cancel{0} \text{ cm}^3}{2{,}4\cancel{0}\cancel{0} \text{ cm}^2}$$

$$= 47.5 \text{ cm}$$

```
  1 2 6
-   1 2
-------
  1 1 4
```

```
        4 7. 5
24) 1,1 4 0
   -   9 6
   -------
       1 8 0
     - 1 6 8
     -------
         1 2 0
       - 1 2 0
       -------
               0
```

The depth of water in the tank will be **47.5 cm**.

Answer: (a) _____ **52.5 cm** _____

(b) _____ **47.5 cm** _____

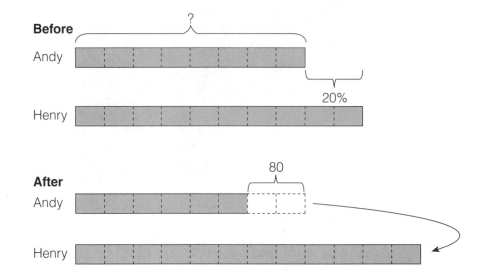

2 equal parts are 80 marbles.

$$80 \div 2 = 40$$

Therefore, each part is 40.

$$8 \times 40 = 320$$

Andy had **320** marbles in the beginning.

Answer: __**320 marbles**__

Solution to Question 5

Use the guess-and-check method.

Number of pirate ship rides	Cost	Number of merry-go-round rides	Cost	Total Cost
4	4 × $0.60 = $2.40	4	4 × $0.90 = $3.60	$2.40 + $3.60 = $6.00
3	3 × $0.60 = $1.80	5	5 × $0.90 = $4.50	$1.80 + $4.50 = $6.30

Lily took **3** pirate ship rides.

Answer: **3 pirate ship rides**

Solution to Question 6

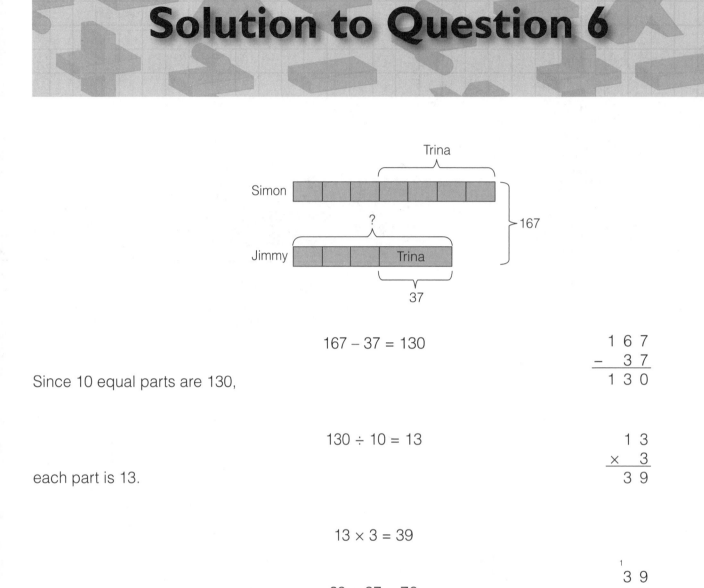

$$167 - 37 = 130$$

$$\begin{array}{r} 1\ 6\ 7 \\ -\ \ 3\ 7 \\ \hline 1\ 3\ 0 \end{array}$$

Since 10 equal parts are 130,

$$130 \div 10 = 13$$

$$\begin{array}{r} 1\ 3 \\ \times\ \ \ 3 \\ \hline 3\ 9 \end{array}$$

each part is 13.

$$13 \times 3 = 39$$

$$39 + 37 = 76$$

$$\begin{array}{r} {}^{1}\ \ \ \\ 3\ 9 \\ +\ 3\ 7 \\ \hline 7\ 6 \end{array}$$

Jimmy had **76** stamps in the beginning.

Answer: **76 stamps**

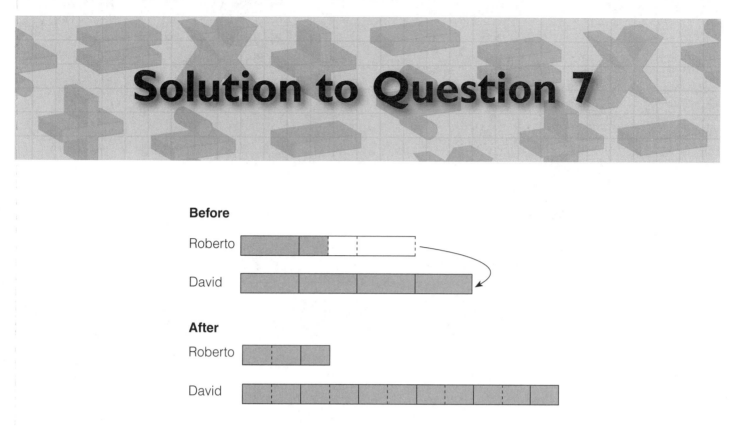

Before

Roberto

David

After

Roberto

David

Using the illustration,

Roberto : David

3 : 11

the ratio of Roberto's cards to David's cards will be **3 : 11**.

Answer: **3 : 11**

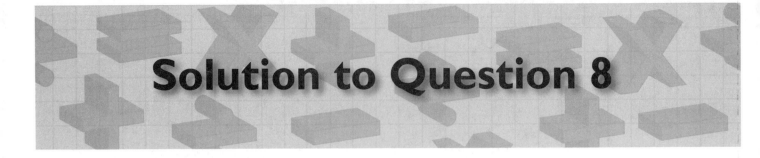

Before

Boys

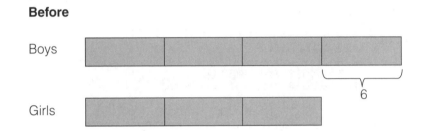

6

Girls

Since each part is 6,

$$Boys : 6 \times 4 = 24$$
$$Girls : 6 \times 3 = 18$$

there are 24 boys and 18 girls in the beginning.

$$18 + 2 = 20$$

There will be 20 girls if another 2 girls join the school choir.

$$Boys : Girls$$
$$24 : 20$$
$$12 : 10$$
$$6 : 5$$

The new ratio of boys to girls will be **6 : 5**.

Answer: _____ **6 : 5** _____

Solution to Question 9

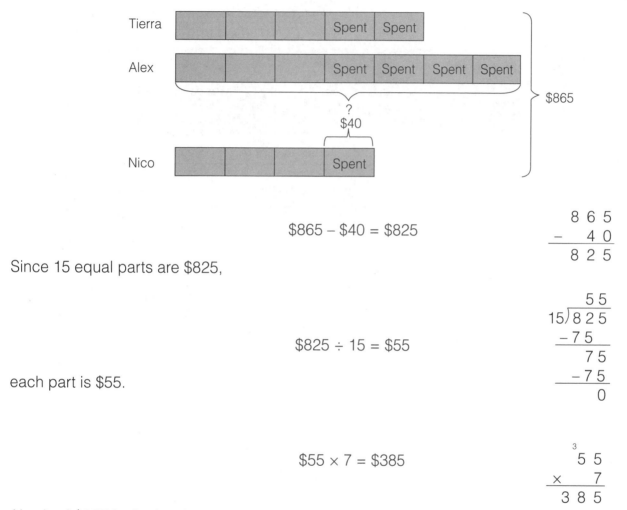

$$\$865 - \$40 = \$825$$

$$\begin{array}{r} 8\;6\;5 \\ -\quad 4\;0 \\ \hline 8\;2\;5 \end{array}$$

Since 15 equal parts are $825,

$$\$825 \div 15 = \$55$$

$$\begin{array}{r} 5\;5 \\ 15\overline{)8\;2\;5} \\ -7\;5 \\ \hline 7\;5 \\ -7\;5 \\ \hline 0 \end{array}$$

each part is $55.

$$\$55 \times 7 = \$385$$

$$\begin{array}{r} {}^{3}\,5\;5 \\ \times\quad 7 \\ \hline 3\;8\;5 \end{array}$$

Alex had **$385** in the beginning.

Answer: **$385**

Use the guess-and-check method.

Number of blue balls	Number of red balls	Total number of red and blue bowling balls	Difference in mass
15	15	30	(15 × 9 lb.) − (15 × 8 lb.) = 135 lb. − 120 lb. = 15 lb.
16	14	30	(16 × 9 lb.) − (14 × 8 lb.) = 144 lb. − 112 lb. = 32 lb.
17	**13**	**30**	**(17 × 9 lb.) − (13 × 8 lb.)** **= 153 lb. − 104 lb.** **= 49 lb.**

She has **13** red balls.

Answer: **13 red balls**

Solution to Question 11

$$\frac{3}{7} + \frac{1}{3} = \frac{9}{21} + \frac{7}{21} = \frac{16}{21}$$

$$1 - \frac{16}{21} = \frac{21}{21} - \frac{16}{21} = \frac{5}{21}$$

$\frac{5}{21}$ of the T-shirts were yellow.

$\frac{9}{21}$ (9 parts) of the T-shirts were red, and $\frac{7}{21}$ (7 parts) of the T-shirts were blue.

$$9 \text{ parts} - 7 \text{ parts} = 2 \text{ parts}$$

There were 20 more red T-shirts than blue T-shirts.

$$2 \text{ parts} = 20$$
$$1 \text{ part} = 20 \div 2$$
$$= 10$$

$\frac{5}{21}$ (5 parts) of the T-shirts were yellow.

$$5 \times 10 = 50$$

There were **50** yellow T-shirts.

Answer: __50 yellow T-shirts__

Solution to Question 12

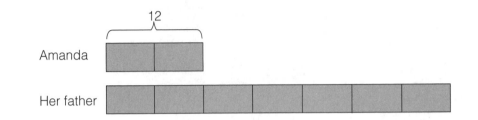

Since 2 equal parts are 12,

each part is 6.

$$12 \div 2 = 6$$

$$7 \times 6 = 42$$

Amanda's father is 42 years old.

$$42 - 12 = 30$$

The difference between Amanda's age and her father's age is 30 years.

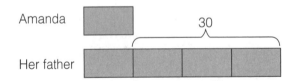

Using the difference in their ages, 3 equal parts are 30.

$$30 \div 3 = 10$$

Each part is 10.

Amanda was 10 years old when her father was 4 times as old as her.

$$12 - 10 = 2$$

Amanda's father was 4 times as old as Amanda **2** years ago.

Answer: __**2 years ago**__

Solution to Question 13

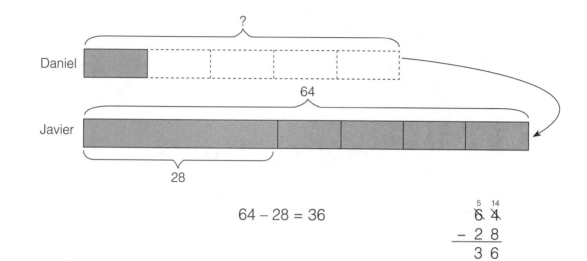

$$64 - 28 = 36$$

$$\begin{array}{r} {\scriptstyle 5}{\scriptstyle 14} \\ \cancel{6}\ \cancel{4} \\ -\ 2\ 8 \\ \hline 3\ 6 \end{array}$$

Since 4 equal parts are 36,

$$36 \div 4 = 9$$

each part is 9.

$$9 \times 5 = 45$$

Daniel had **45** stickers in the beginning.

Answer: **45 stickers**

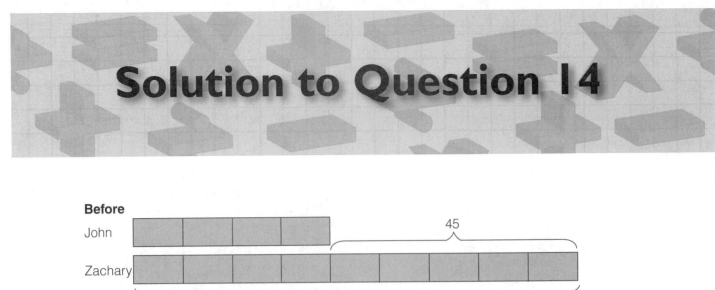

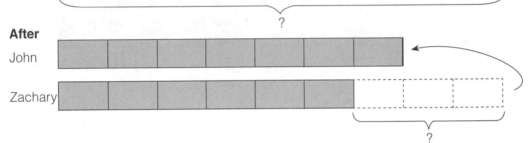

(a)   Since 5 equal parts are 45,

$$45 \div 5 = 9$$

each part is 9.

$$9 \times 9 = 81$$

Zachary had **81** postcards in the beginning.

(b) $$9 \times 3 = 27$$

Zachary gave **27** postcards to John.

Answer: (a) __81 postcards__

(b) __27 postcards__

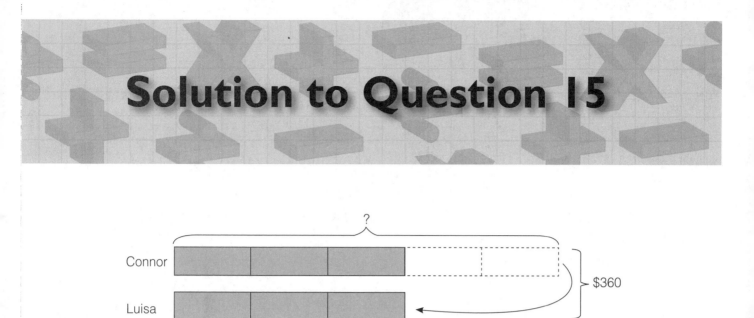

Since 6 equal parts are $360,

$$\$360 \div 6 = \$60$$

each part is $60.

$$\$60 \times 5 = \$300$$

Connor had **$300** in the beginning.

Answer: **$300**

Solution to Question 16

$$\frac{\cancel{60}}{\cancel{100}} \times \cancel{840} = 504$$

There were 504 adults.

$$
\begin{array}{r}
{}^{2} \\
8\ 4 \\
\times \quad 6 \\
\hline
5\ 0\ 4
\end{array}
$$

$$840 - 504 = 336$$

There were 336 children.

$$
\begin{array}{r}
{}^{3}{}^{10} \\
8\ \cancel{4}\ \cancel{0} \\
-\ 5\ 0\ 4 \\
\hline
3\ 3\ 6
\end{array}
$$

The number of adults increased to 70% after some boys left.

Since 7 equal parts are 504,

$$504 \div 7 = 72$$

each part is 72.

$$
\begin{array}{r}
7\ 2 \\
7\overline{)5\ 0\ 4} \\
-4\ 9 \\
\hline
1\ 4 \\
-1\ 4 \\
\hline
0
\end{array}
$$

$$72 \times 3 = 216$$

$$
\begin{array}{r}
7\ 2 \\
\times \quad 3 \\
\hline
2\ 1\ 6
\end{array}
$$

216 children remained at the wedding dinner.

$$336 - 216 = 120$$

$$
\begin{array}{r}
3\ 3\ 6 \\
-\ 2\ 1\ 6 \\
\hline
1\ 2\ 0
\end{array}
$$

120 boys left before the dessert was served.

Answer: **120 boys**

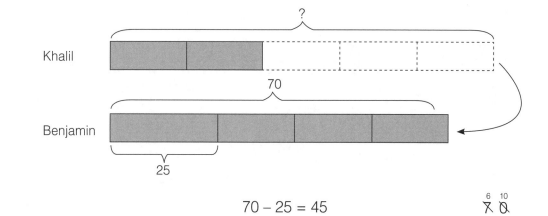

$$70 - 25 = 45$$

Since 3 equal parts are 45,

$$45 \div 3 = 15$$

each part is 15.

$$15 \times 5 = 75$$

Khalil had **75** rocks in the beginning.

Answer: __**75 rocks**__

Solution to Question 18

16

Folders	Folders

Rulers

36 items in total
$20.20

$$36 - 16 = 20$$

Since 2 equal parts are 20,

$$20 \div 2 = 10$$

each part is 10.

There were 10 rulers.

$$10 + 16 = 26$$

There were 26 folders.

?

Folder

Ruler

$0.50

Since each folder cost $0.50 more,

$$26 \times \$0.50 = \$13.00$$

26 folders cost $13 more.

$$\$20.20 - \$13.00 = \$7.20$$

$$\$7.20 \div 36 = 720¢ \div 36 = 20¢$$

Each ruler cost 20¢.

$$20¢ + 50¢ = 70¢$$

Each folder cost **70¢**.

```
  1
  3
  0.50
×   26
  300
+100
13.00
```

```
 1 10
2̸0̸.20
-13.00
  7.20
```

```
      20
36)720
    -72
       0
      -0
       0
```

Answer: __70¢ or $0.70__

Solution to Question 19

44 legs ÷ 4 legs = 11 pet rabbits

Jackson has 11 more pet rabbits than pet birds.

14 pets – 11 pet rabbits = 3 pets

A rabbit has 4 legs, and a bird has 2 legs.

1 rabbit and 2 birds are the remaining 3 pets.

He has **2** pet birds.

Answer: **2 pet birds**

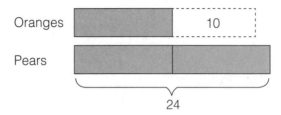

$$24 \div 2 = 12$$

He had 12 oranges in the end.

$$12 + 10 = 22$$

He had 22 oranges in the beginning.

$$
\begin{array}{ccc}
\text{Oranges} & : & \text{Pears} \\
22 & : & 24 \\
11 & : & 12
\end{array}
$$

The ratio of oranges to pears in the beginning was **11 : 12**.

Answer: _____**11 : 12**_____

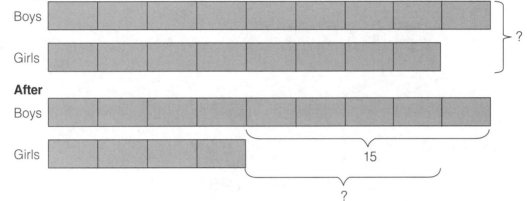

(a)　Since 5 equal parts are 15,

$$15 \div 5 = 3$$

each part is 3.

$$17 \times 3 = 51$$

$$\begin{array}{r} \overset{2}{1}\,7 \\ \times\quad 3 \\ \hline 5\,1 \end{array}$$

51 children were in the classroom in the beginning.

(b)　　　　　　　　　　　　$$4 \times 3 = 12$$

12 girls left the classroom.

Answer: (a) __**51 children**__

(b) __**12 girls**__

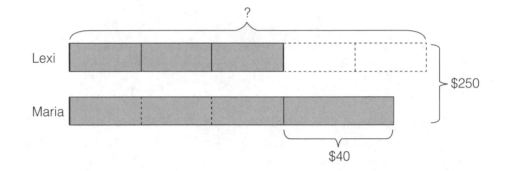

$$\$250 - \$40 = \$210$$

Since 8 equal parts are $210,

$$\$210 \div 8 = \$26.25$$

each part is $26.25.

```
        26.25
     8)210
      -16
        50
       -48
         20
        -16
          40
         -40
           0
```

$$\$26.25 \times 5 = \$131.25$$

```
    ³2⁶.¹2²5
  ×      5
   131.25
```

Lexi had **$131.25** in the beginning.

Answer: **$131.25**

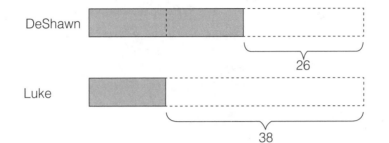

$$38 - 26 = 12$$

$$\begin{array}{r} 3\ 8 \\ -\ 2\ 6 \\ \hline 1\ 2 \end{array}$$

Each part is 12.

$$12 + 38 = 50$$

$$\begin{array}{r} \overset{1}{1}\ 2 \\ +\ 3\ 8 \\ \hline 5\ 0 \end{array}$$

Each of them had **50** stickers in the beginning.

Answer: __**50 stickers**__

Since there were 75 pebbles in 3 boxes,

$$75 \div 3 = 25$$

$$\begin{array}{r} 25 \\ 3\overline{)75} \\ -6 \\ \hline 15 \\ -15 \\ \hline 0 \end{array}$$

there should be 25 pebbles in each box in the end.

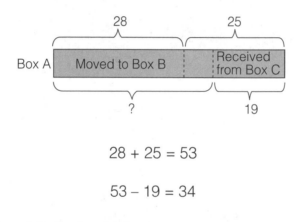

$$28 + 25 = 53$$

$$53 - 19 = 34$$

There were **34** pebbles in Box A in the beginning.

Answer: **34 pebbles**

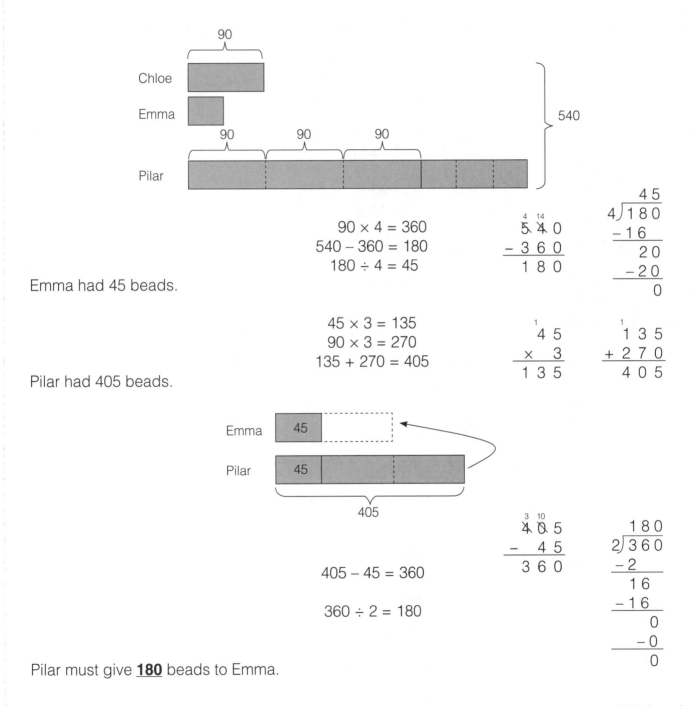

$90 \times 4 = 360$
$540 - 360 = 180$
$180 \div 4 = 45$

Emma had 45 beads.

$45 \times 3 = 135$
$90 \times 3 = 270$
$135 + 270 = 405$

Pilar had 405 beads.

$405 - 45 = 360$

$360 \div 2 = 180$

Pilar must give **180** beads to Emma.

Answer: ___**180 beads**___

Solution to Question 26

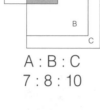

A : B : C
7 : 8 : 10

Since $\frac{1}{4}$ of Square B is shaded,

$$\frac{1}{4} \times 8 = 2$$

the shaded area of Square B is 2 parts.

$$7 - 2 = 5$$

The unshaded area of Square A is 5 parts.

$$8 - 2 = 6$$

The unshaded area of Square B is 6 parts.

$$10 - 8 = 2$$

The unshaded area of Square C is 2 parts.

$$5 + 6 + 2 = 13$$

Shaded area : Unshaded areas

2 : 13

The ratio of the shaded area to the unshaded areas is **2 : 13**.

Answer: **2 : 13**

(a)

$$10 \times 50 = 500$$

There were 500 oranges altogether.

$$\frac{65}{100} \times 500 = 325$$

$$325 \div 5 = 65$$

He sold 325 oranges, or 65 groups of 5 oranges.

$$65 \times \$1.20 = \$78$$

```
    2
   6 5
 ×   5
   3 2 5

   1 1
   1.2 0
 ×   6 5
   6 0 0
 + 7 2 0
  7 8.0 0
```

```
      6 5
  5)3 2 5
   - 3 0
      2 5
    - 2 5
        0
```

Mr. Santiago earned **$78**.

(b)

$$500 - 325 = 175$$

$$\frac{8}{100} \times 175 = \frac{1{,}400}{100} = 14$$

$$175 - 14 = 161$$

```
   4 9 10
   5̶ 0̶ 0
 - 3 2 5
   1 7 5
```

```
    6  4
    1 7 5
 ×      8
  1, 4 0 0
```

There were 161 oranges left.

$$\$24.15 \div 161 = 2{,}415¢ \div 161$$
$$= 15¢$$

```
          1 5
 161)2, 4 1 5
    - 1 6 1
        8 0 5
      - 8 0 5
            0
```

He charged **15¢** for each orange.

Answer: (a) _____**$78**_____

(b) __**15¢ or $0.15**__

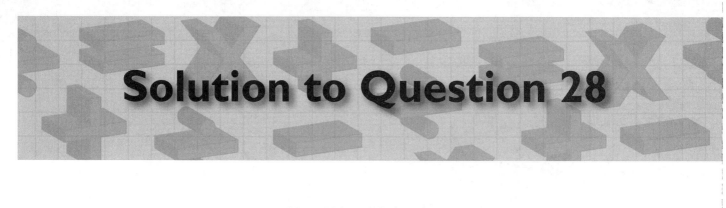

$$30 \times 30¢ = 900¢ = \$9$$

$$\$9 + \$3 = \$12$$

Jason earns $12 for every 30 carrots he sells.

$$\$555 \div \$12 = 46.25$$

(Round off to the nearest whole number.)

$$
\begin{array}{r}
46.25 \\
12\overline{)555} \\
-48 \\
\hline
75 \\
-72 \\
\hline
30 \\
-24 \\
\hline
60 \\
-60 \\
\hline
0
\end{array}
$$

He needs to sell at least 46 groups of 30 carrots.

$$46 \times \$12 = \$552$$

$$\$555 - \$552 = \$3$$

$$\$3 \div 30¢ = 300¢ \div 30¢ = 10$$

$$
\begin{array}{r}
{}^{1}\,46 \\
\times\;\;12 \\
\hline
92 \\
+\,{}^{1}46\;\; \\
\hline
552
\end{array}
$$

He needs to sell another 10 carrots.

$$46 \times 30 = 1,380$$

$$1,380 + 10 = 1,390$$

He must sell **1,390** carrots in order to earn $555.

$$
\begin{array}{r}
{}^{1}\,46 \\
\times\;\;30 \\
\hline
00 \\
+\,138\;\; \\
\hline
1,380
\end{array}
$$

Answer: __**1,390 carrots**__

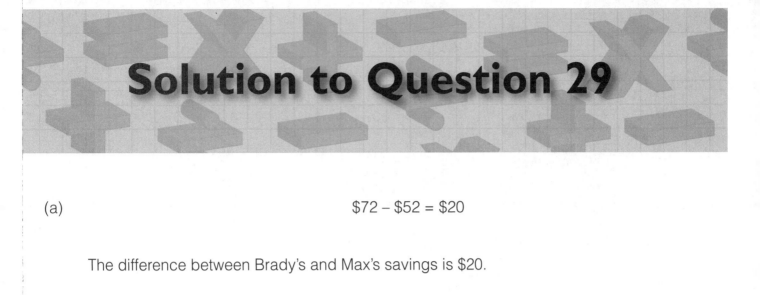

(a)

$$\$72 - \$52 = \$20$$

The difference between Brady's and Max's savings is $20.

Brady gets $2.50 more than Max every week.

$$\$20 \div \$2.50 = 2{,}000¢ \div 250¢$$
$$= 200 \div 25$$
$$= 8$$

$$\begin{array}{r} 8 \\ 25\overline{)200} \\ -200 \\ \hline 0 \end{array}$$

It takes Brady **8** weeks to save $72.

(b)

$$\$52 \div 8 = \$6.50$$

$$\begin{array}{r} 6.5 \\ 8\overline{)52} \\ -48 \\ \hline 40 \\ -40 \\ \hline 0 \end{array}$$

Max saves $6.50 in a week.

$$\$6.50 + \$6 = \$12.50$$

$$\begin{array}{r} 6.5 \\ + 6 0 \\ \hline 1 2.5 \end{array}$$

Max gets **$12.50** every week.

Answer: (a) ___**8 weeks**___

(b) ___**$12.50**___

Since each hat cost $5,

$$3 \times \$5 = \$15$$

3 hats cost $15.

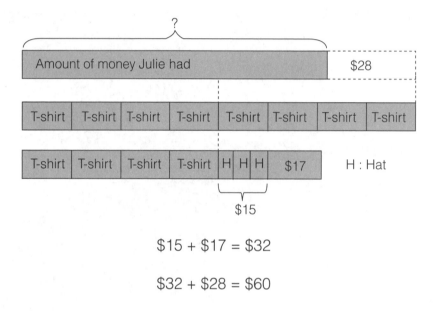

$$\$15 + \$17 = \$32$$

$$\$32 + \$28 = \$60$$

Since 4 T-shirts cost $60,

$$\$60 + \$15 + \$17 = \$92$$

she had **$92** in the beginning.

Answer: _____**$92**_____

Solution to Question 31

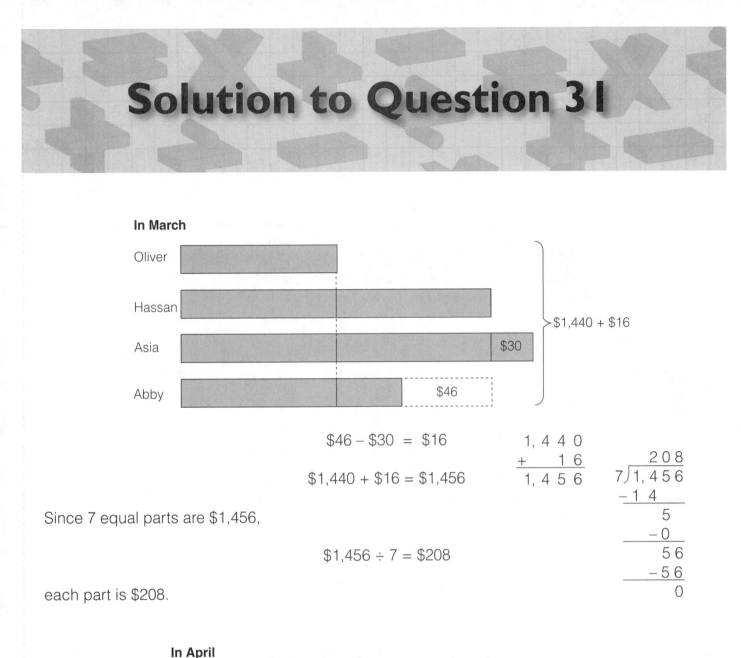

In March

Oliver

Hassan

Asia $30

Abby $46

$1,440 + $16

$46 − $30 = $16

$1,440 + $16 = $1,456

Since 7 equal parts are $1,456,

$1,456 ÷ 7 = $208

each part is $208.

$$\begin{array}{r} 1,4\,4\,0 \\ +\quad\ 1\,6 \\ \hline 1,4\,5\,6 \end{array}$$

$$\begin{array}{r} 208 \\ 7\overline{)1,456} \\ -14 \\ \hline 5 \\ -0 \\ \hline 56 \\ -56 \\ \hline 0 \end{array}$$

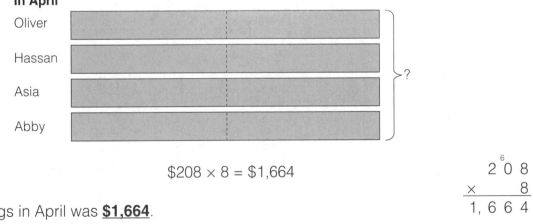

In April

Oliver

Hassan

Asia

Abby

?

$208 × 8 = $1,664

Their total savings in April was **$1,664**.

$$\begin{array}{r} 2\overset{6}{0}8 \\ \times\quad\ 8 \\ \hline 1,664 \end{array}$$

Answer: **$1,664**

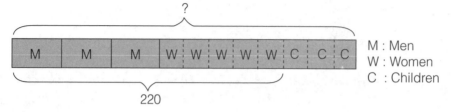

Each part of the number of men is equal to 2 equal parts of the number of women.

$$6 \text{ parts} + 5 \text{ parts} = 11 \text{ parts}$$

$$11 \text{ parts} = 220$$
$$1 \text{ part} = 220 \div 11$$
$$= 20$$

$$11 \text{ parts} + 3 \text{ parts} = 14 \text{ parts}$$
$$14 \text{ parts} = 20 \times 14$$
$$= 280$$

```
    2 0
 ×  1 4
    8 0
+ 2 0
  2 8 0
```

__280__ people live in the apartment building.

Answer: __280 people__

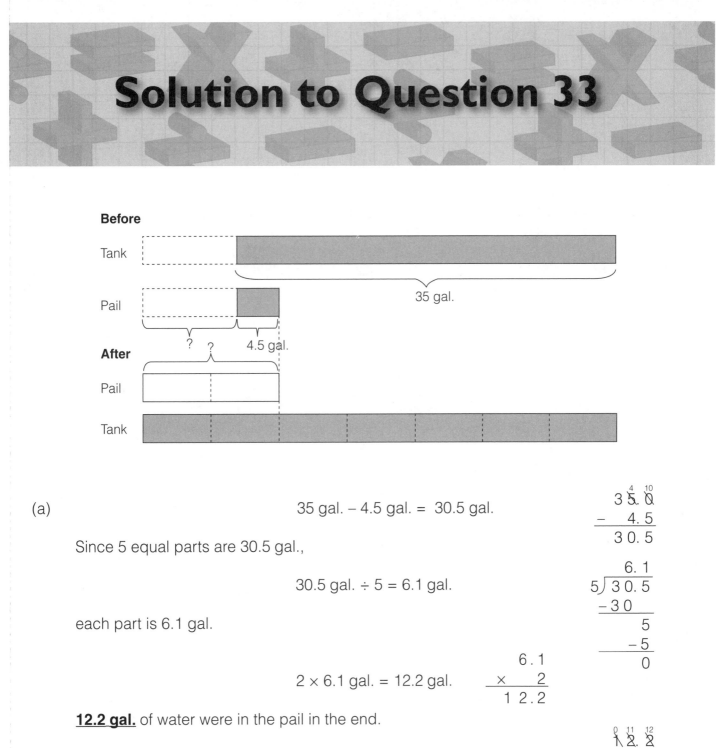

(a)   35 gal. − 4.5 gal. = 30.5 gal.

Since 5 equal parts are 30.5 gal.,

30.5 gal. ÷ 5 = 6.1 gal.

each part is 6.1 gal.

2 × 6.1 gal. = 12.2 gal.

12.2 gal. of water were in the pail in the end.

(b)   12.2 gal. − 4.5 gal. = 7.7 gal.

7.7 gal. of water were poured into the pail.

Answer: (a) ___**12.2 gal.**___

(b) ___**7.7 gal.**___

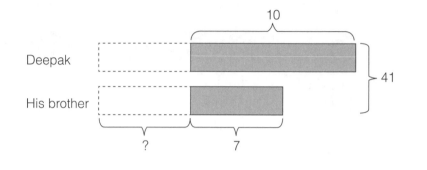

$$10 + 7 = 17$$

$$41 - 17 = 24$$

Since 2 equal parts are 24,

$$24 \div 2 = 12$$

each part is 12.

Their total age will be 41 years old in **12** years.

Answer: **12 years**

1 one-dollar coin equals 2 fifty-cent coins.

$$6 \text{ one-dollar coins} = 6 \times 2$$
$$= 12 \text{ fifty-cent coins}$$

One-dollar : Fifty-cent
6 : 12
1 : 2

The ratio of 6 one-dollar coins to 12 fifty-cent coins was 1 : 2.

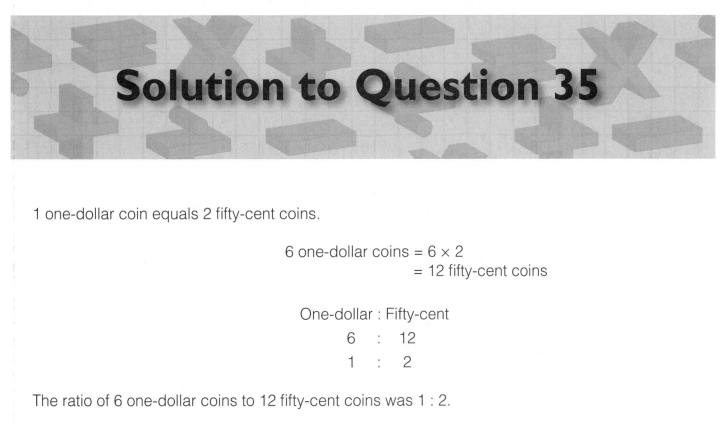

Since 1 part of the one-dollar coins is $6,

$$\$6 \times 3 = \$18$$

the amount of money in one-dollar coins is $18.

Since 2 parts of the fifty-cent coins are $6,

$$\$6 \times 2 = \$12$$

the amount of money in fifty-cent coins is $12.

$$\$18 + \$12 = \$30$$

The total amount of money in the box was **$30**.

Answer: _____**$30**_____

Before

There were 500 ducks and 300 chickens.

After

The farmer bought 10 more ducks and 75 more chickens.

$$100\% - 12\% = 88\%$$

$$\frac{88}{100} \times 500 = 440$$

$$
\begin{array}{r}
\overset{4}{8}\,8 \\
\times \quad 5 \\
\hline
4\,4\,0
\end{array}
$$

There were 440 ducks left.

$$100\% + 15\% = 115\%$$

$$\frac{115}{100} \times 300 = 345$$

$$
\begin{array}{r}
1\,\overset{1}{1}\,5 \\
\times \quad 3 \\
\hline
3\,4\,5
\end{array}
$$

There were 345 chickens left.

(a)

$$500 + 10 = 510$$

$$510 - 440 = 70$$

$$
\begin{array}{r}
\overset{4}{5}\,\overset{11}{\cancel{1}}\,0 \\
-\ 4\,4\,0 \\
\hline
7\,0
\end{array}
$$

The farmer gave away **70** ducks.

(b)

$$100 - 70 = 30$$

He gave away **30** chickens.

Answer: (a) __**70 ducks**__

(b) __**30 chickens**__

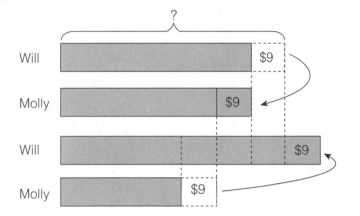

$$\$9 \times 4 = \$36$$

$$\$36 \times 2 = \$72$$

$$\begin{array}{r} {}^{1}3\ 6 \\ \times\quad 2 \\ \hline 7\ 2 \end{array}$$

Will will have $72 if Molly gives him $9.

$$\$72 - \$9 = \$63$$

$$\begin{array}{r} {}^{6}\ {}^{12}\\ \cancel{7}\ \cancel{2} \\ -\quad 9 \\ \hline 6\ 3 \end{array}$$

Will has **$63** in the beginning.

Answer: _____**$63**_____

Using the lowest common multiple of 2 and 3 to make the ratio of angelfish the same, the new ratio is as follows:

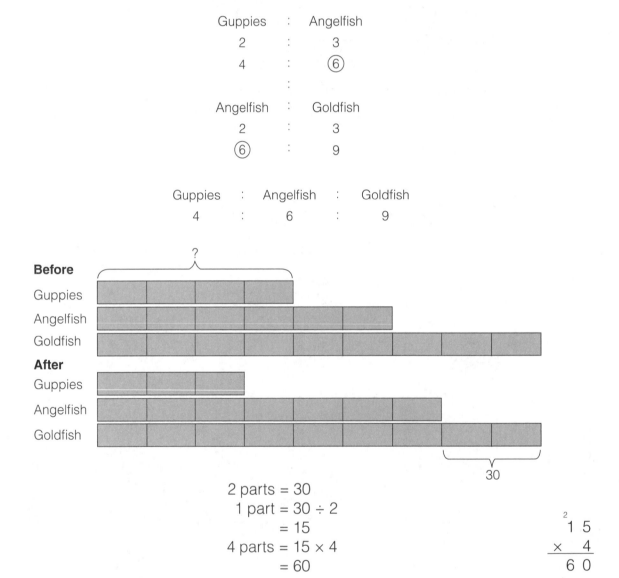

	Guppies	:	Angelfish
	2	:	3
	4	:	⑥

	Angelfish	:	Goldfish
	2	:	3
	⑥	:	9

Guppies	:	Angelfish	:	Goldfish
4	:	6	:	9

Before
Guppies
Angelfish
Goldfish

After
Guppies
Angelfish
Goldfish

?

30

2 parts = 30
1 part = 30 ÷ 2
= 15
4 parts = 15 × 4
= 60

$$\begin{array}{r}\overset{2}{1}\,5 \\ \times\quad 4 \\ \hline 6\,0\end{array}$$

There were **60** guppies in the shop in the beginning.

Answer: ___**60 guppies**___

Solution to Question 39

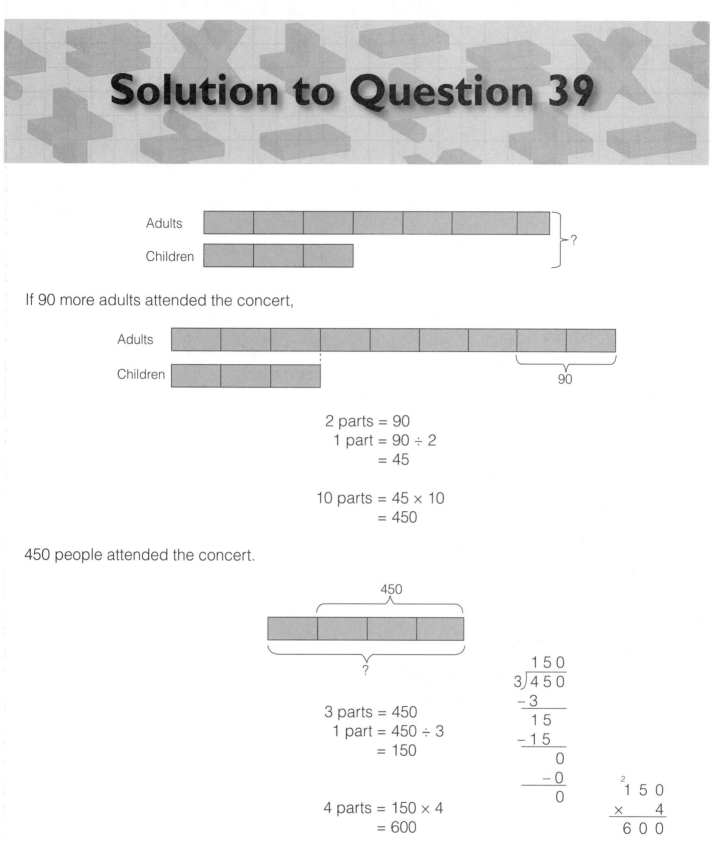

If 90 more adults attended the concert,

2 parts = 90
1 part = 90 ÷ 2
= 45

10 parts = 45 × 10
= 450

450 people attended the concert.

3 parts = 450
1 part = 450 ÷ 3
= 150

$$
\begin{array}{r}
150 \\
3\overline{)450} \\
-3 \\
\hline
15 \\
-15 \\
\hline
0 \\
-0 \\
\hline
0
\end{array}
$$

4 parts = 150 × 4
= 600

$$
\begin{array}{r}
^{2}150 \\
\times4 \\
\hline
600
\end{array}
$$

There were **600** seats in the concert hall.

Answer: **600 seats**

$$5 - 3 = 2$$

The unshaded area for Square B is 2 parts.

$$17 - 9 = 8$$

The unshaded area for Square A is 8 parts.

Multiply the parts of the shaded area of Square B by 3 to make the ratio of the shaded areas of Squares A and B common.

Shaded area of A	:	Unshaded area of A
⑨	:	8

Shaded area of B	:	Unshaded area of B
3	:	2
⑨	:	6

$$8 + 6 = 14$$

The total unshaded areas equal 14 parts.

Shaded area	:	Total unshaded areas
9	:	14

The ratio of the shaded area to the total unshaded areas of the figure is **9 : 14**.

Answer: _____**9 : 14**_____

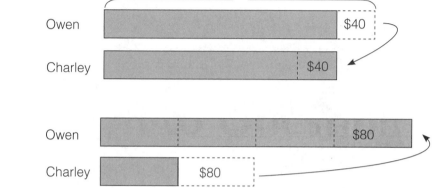

Since each part is $80,

$$\$80 \times 4 = \$320$$

Owen has $320 in the end.

$$\$320 - \$80 = \$240$$

Owen has **$240** in the beginning.

Answer: **$240**

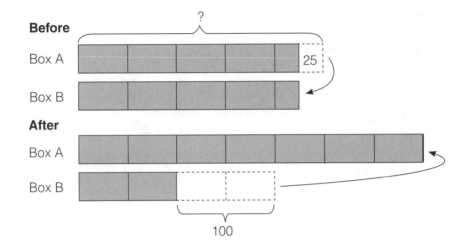

Since 2 parts are 100,

$$100 \div 2 = 50$$

each part is 50.

$$50 \times 5 = 250$$

The original number of dimes in Box A was **250**.

Answer: **250 dimes**

Solution to Question 43

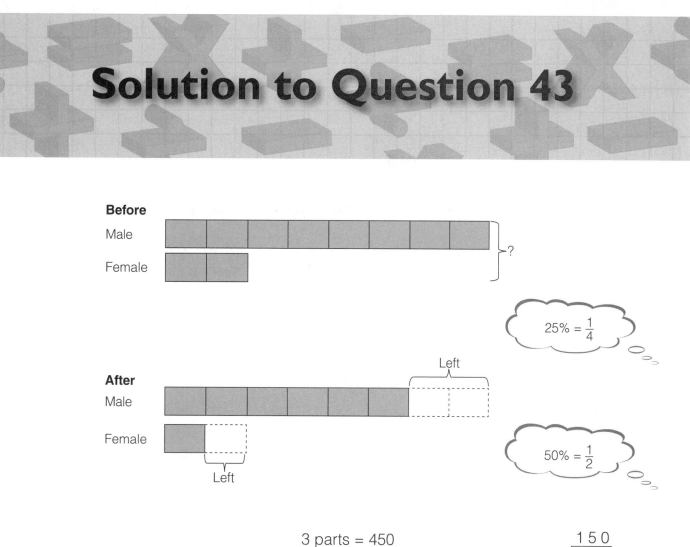

Before

Male

Female

?

$25\% = \dfrac{1}{4}$

Left

After

Male

Female

Left

$50\% = \dfrac{1}{2}$

3 parts = 450

1 part = 450 ÷ 3
= 150

10 parts = 150 × 10
= 1,500

```
        1 5 0
  3 ) 4 5 0
     − 3
      1 5
     − 1 5
         0
       − 0
         0
```

The number of members in the tennis club in the beginning was **1,500**.

Answer: **1,500 members**

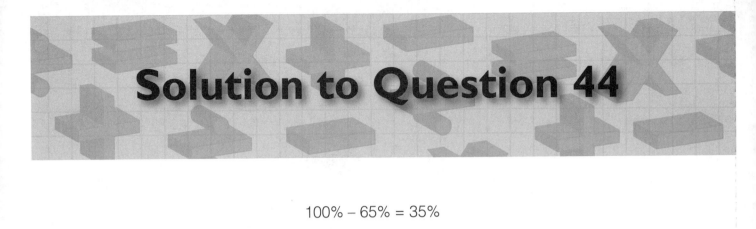

$$100\% - 65\% = 35\%$$

35% of the students took buses to school.

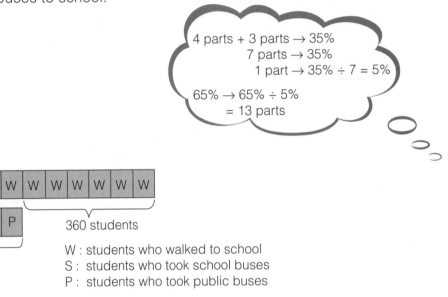

4 parts + 3 parts → 35%
7 parts → 35%
1 part → 35% ÷ 7 = 5%
65% → 65% ÷ 5%
= 13 parts

360 students

W : students who walked to school
S : students who took school buses
P : students who took public buses

$$6 \text{ parts} = 360$$
$$1 \text{ part} = 360 \div 6$$
$$= 60$$

$$3 \text{ parts} = 60 \times 3$$
$$= 180$$

180 students took public buses to school.

Answer: **180 students**

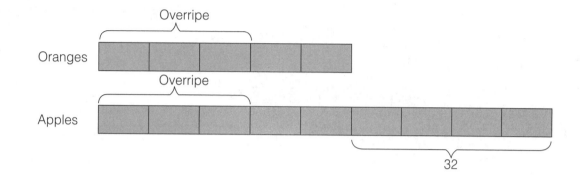

Since 4 equal parts are 32,

$$32 \div 4 = 8$$

each part is 8.

$$8 \times 6 = 48$$

There are **48** pieces of overripe fruit.

Answer: **48 pieces of overripe fruit**

Solution to Question 46

$$38 - 8 = 30$$

Since 6 equal parts are 30,

$$30 \div 6 = 5$$

each part is 5.

(a)
$$5 + 4 = 9$$

His son is **9** years old this year.

(b)
$$38 - 9 = 29$$

Mr. Bellini is **29** years old this year.

Answer: (a) **9 years old**

(b) **29 years old**

Solution to Question 47

Interval Time	Filling of water from Tap A	Draining of water from Tap B
After 2 min.	6 L × 2 = 12 L	–
After another 2 min.	6 L × 2 = 12 L	2 L × 2 = 4 L
After another 2 min.	6 L × 2 = 12 L	2 L × 2 = 4 L
After another 2 min.	6 L × 2 = 12 L	2 L × 2 = 4 L
Total	48 L	12 L

$$48 \text{ L} - 12 \text{ L} = 36 \text{ L}$$

There were 36 L of water in the tank after 8 minutes.

$$\text{Volume} = \text{Length} \times \text{Width} \times \text{Height}$$

$$36 \text{ L} = 50 \text{ cm} \times 40 \text{ cm} \times \text{Height}$$

$1 \text{ L} = 1000 \text{ cm}^3$

$$36{,}000 \text{ cm}^3 = 2{,}000 \text{ cm}^2 \times \text{Height}$$
$$\text{Height} = 36{,}000 \div 2{,}000$$
$$= 36 \div 2$$
$$= 18 \text{ cm}$$

The depth of water left in the tank was **18 cm**.

```
      5 0
   ×  4 0
   ------
      0 0
  + 2 0 0
   ------
   2,0 0 0
```

```
       1 8
   2 ) 3 6
      - 2
      ----
       1 6
      -1 6
      ----
         0
```

Answer: _____**18 cm**_____

Solution to Question 48

(a)

Red : Blue	Blue : Green
5 : 2	3 : 5

Use the lowest common multiple of 2 and 3 to make the ratio of blue markers common.

Red : Blue	Blue : Green
15 : ⑥	⑥ : 10

The ratio of red markers to blue markers to green markers was **15 : 6 : 10**.

(b)

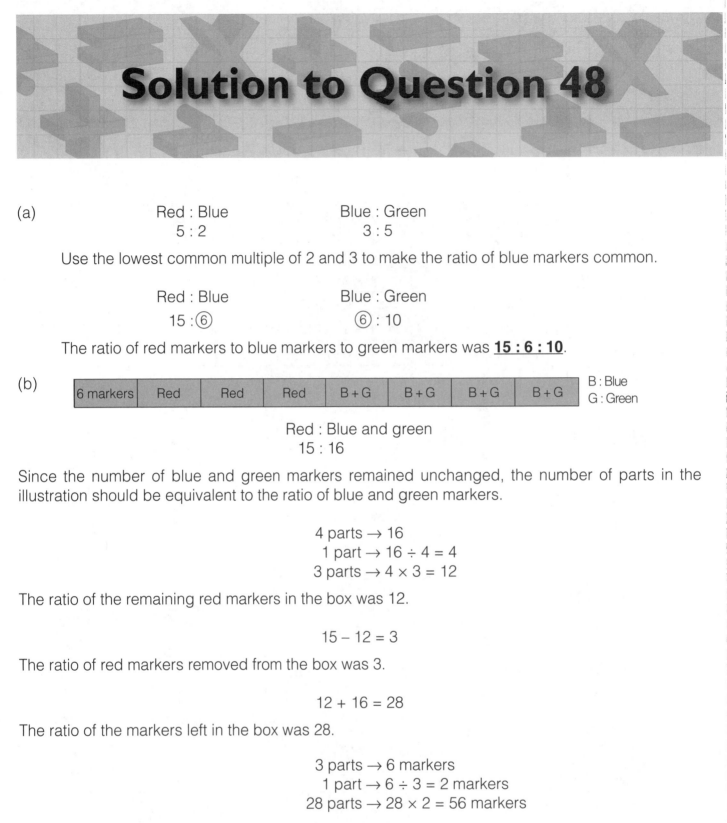

Red : Blue and green
15 : 16

Since the number of blue and green markers remained unchanged, the number of parts in the illustration should be equivalent to the ratio of blue and green markers.

$$4 \text{ parts} \rightarrow 16$$
$$1 \text{ part} \rightarrow 16 \div 4 = 4$$
$$3 \text{ parts} \rightarrow 4 \times 3 = 12$$

The ratio of the remaining red markers in the box was 12.

$$15 - 12 = 3$$

The ratio of red markers removed from the box was 3.

$$12 + 16 = 28$$

The ratio of the markers left in the box was 28.

$$3 \text{ parts} \rightarrow 6 \text{ markers}$$
$$1 \text{ part} \rightarrow 6 \div 3 = 2 \text{ markers}$$
$$28 \text{ parts} \rightarrow 28 \times 2 = 56 \text{ markers}$$

56 markers were left in the box.

Answer: (a) ____**15 : 6 : 10**____

(b) ____**56 markers**____

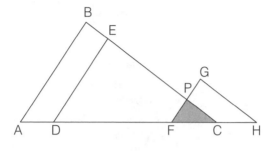

$$20\% \times 5 = \frac{20}{100} \times 5 = \frac{100}{100} = 1$$

1 part of DEC is shaded.

Since the shaded area is shared among triangles DEC and FGH,

$$3 \text{ parts} - 1 \text{ part} = 2 \text{ parts}$$

CPGH is 2 parts.

Since triangle ABC is 7 parts,

$$ABC + CPGH = 7 \text{ parts} + 2 \text{ parts} = 9 \text{ parts}$$

the total area of the whole figure is 9 parts.

$$9 \text{ parts} - 1 \text{ part} = 8 \text{ parts}$$

The unshaded area is 8 parts.

$$\frac{\text{Unshaded area}}{\text{Total area}} \times 100\%$$
$$= \frac{8}{9} \times 100\%$$
$$= \frac{800}{9} = 88\frac{8}{9}\%$$

$$\begin{array}{r} 88 \\ 9\overline{)800} \\ -72 \\ \hline 80 \\ -72 \\ \hline 8 \end{array}$$

$\underline{88\frac{8}{9}\%}$ of the figure is unshaded.

Answer:

Town A   ?   Town B

12 P.M.   3 P.M.

Carter (at 50 mph)

(a)

$$\text{Distance} = \text{Speed} \times \text{Time}$$
$$= 50 \text{ mph} \times 3 \text{ hr.}$$
$$= 150 \text{ mi.}$$

$$60\% \rightarrow 150 \text{ mi.}$$
$$1\% \rightarrow 150 \div 60$$
$$= 15 \div 6 = 2.5 \text{ mi.}$$
$$100\% \rightarrow 100 \times 2.5$$
$$= 250 \text{ mi.}$$

```
       2.5
  6) 1 5
    -1 2
       3 0
      -3 0
         0
```

Town A was **250 mi.** from Town B.

(b)

$$100\% - 60\% = 40\%$$
$$40\% \rightarrow 40 \times 2.5 = 100 \text{ mi.}$$

Minh traveled 100 mi.

```
       4 0
    ×  2.5
     2 0 0
   + 8 0
   1 0 0.0
```

$$1500 \text{ hr.} - 1230 \text{ hr.} = 230 \text{ hr.} = 2\frac{1}{2} \text{ hr.}$$

Minh traveled for $2\frac{1}{2}$ hours.

$$\text{Speed} = \text{Distance} \div \text{Time}$$
$$= 100 \text{ mi.} \div 2\frac{1}{2} \text{ hr.}$$
$$= 100 \text{ mi.} \div \frac{5}{2} \text{ hr.}$$
$$= \overset{20}{100} \text{ mi.} \times \frac{2}{\underset{1}{5}} \text{ hr.}$$
$$= 40 \text{ mph}$$

Minh was traveling at **40 mph**.

Answer: (a)   **250 mi.**

(b)   **40 mph**

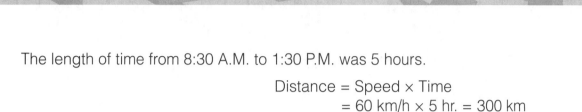

Solution to Question 51

The length of time from 8:30 A.M. to 1:30 P.M. was 5 hours.

$$\text{Distance} = \text{Speed} \times \text{Time}$$
$$= 60 \text{ km/h} \times 5 \text{ hr.} = 300 \text{ km}$$

The total distance was 300 km.

$$\frac{60}{\cancel{100}_1} \times \cancel{300}^3 = 180 \text{ km}$$

$$\text{Time} = \text{Distance} \div \text{Speed}$$
$$= 180 \text{ km} \div 90 \text{ km/h}$$
$$= 18 \text{ km} \div 9 \text{ km/h}$$
$$= 2 \text{ hr.}$$

The distance and time taken for the first 60% of the trip were 180 km and 2 hr. respectively.

$$300 \text{ km} - 180 \text{ km} = 120 \text{ km}$$

The remaining trip was 120 km.

$$\frac{\cancel{25}^5}{\cancel{100}_{\cancel{5}_1}^{8}} \times \cancel{120}^6 \text{ km} = 30 \text{ km}$$

$$\text{Time} = 30 \text{ km} \div 60 \text{ km/h}$$
$$= 0.5 \text{ hr.} = \frac{1}{2} \text{ hr.}$$

The time taken for 25% of the remaining trip was $\frac{1}{2}$ hour.

$$120 \text{ km} - 30 \text{ km} = 90 \text{ km}$$
$$5 \text{ hr.} - 2 \text{ hr.} - \frac{1}{2} \text{ hr.} = 2\frac{1}{2} \text{ hr.}$$

$$\text{Speed} = 90 \text{ km} \div 2\frac{1}{2} \text{ hr.}$$
$$= 90 \text{ km} \div \frac{5}{2} \text{ hr.}$$
$$= \cancel{90}^{18} \times \frac{2}{\cancel{5}_1} = 36 \text{ km/h}$$

His average speed for the remaining part of the trip was **36 km/h**.

$$\begin{array}{r} {}^{2}\cancel{3}\ {}^{10}\cancel{0}\ 0 \\ -\ 1\ 8\ 0 \\ \hline 1\ 2\ 0 \end{array}$$

$$\begin{array}{r} 0.5 \\ 60\overline{)3\ 0} \\ -\ 3\ 0 \\ \hline 3\ 0\ 0 \\ -\ 3\ 0\ 0 \\ \hline 0 \end{array}$$

Answer: __**36 km/h**__

(a)

$$48 \text{ min.} = \frac{48}{60} \text{ hr.}$$
$$= \frac{4}{5} \text{ hr.}$$

Speed = Distance ÷ Time

$$= 40 \text{ mi.} \div \frac{4}{5} \text{ hr.}$$

$$= \overset{10}{4\!\!\!/0} \text{ mi.} \times \frac{5}{\underset{1}{4\!\!\!/}} \text{ hr.}$$

$$= 50 \text{ mph}$$

Time = Distance ÷ Speed
$$= 240 \text{ mi.} \div 50 \text{ mph}$$
$$= 24 \text{ mi.} \div 5 \text{ mph}$$
$$= 4\frac{4}{5} \text{ hr.}$$

$$\frac{4}{\underset{1}{5\!\!\!/}} \times \overset{12}{6\!\!\!/0} = 48 \text{ min.}$$

$$\begin{array}{r} 4 \\ 5\overline{)2\,4} \\ -2\,0 \\ \hline 4 \end{array}$$

$$\begin{array}{r} 1\,2 \\ \times\quad 4 \\ \hline 4\,8 \end{array}$$

Mickey took **4 hr. and 48 min.** to drive to the city.

(b)

$$4 \text{ hr. } 48 \text{ min.} - 48 \text{ min.} = 4 \text{ hr.}$$

Dylan took 4 hours to complete the trip.

$$240 \text{ mi.} \div 4 \text{ hr.} = 60 \text{ mph}$$

$$\begin{array}{r} 6\,0 \\ 4\overline{)2\,4\,0} \\ -2\,4 \\ \hline 0 \\ -0 \\ \hline 0 \end{array}$$

Dylan's driving speed was **60 mph**.

Answer: (a) __**4 hr. and 48 min.**__

(b) __**60 mph**__

Solution to Question 53

Make the amount of money Calvin received 3 parts to eliminate the fractions.

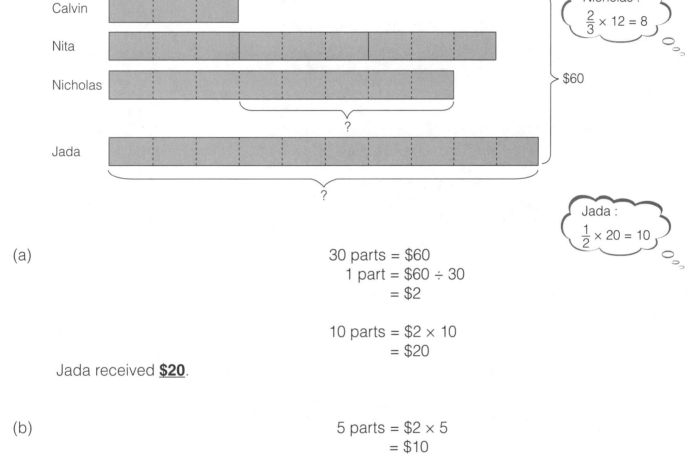

(a)
$$30 \text{ parts} = \$60$$
$$1 \text{ part} = \$60 \div 30$$
$$= \$2$$

$$10 \text{ parts} = \$2 \times 10$$
$$= \$20$$

Jada received **$20**.

(b)
$$5 \text{ parts} = \$2 \times 5$$
$$= \$10$$

Nicholas received **$10** more than Calvin.

Answer: (a) <u>**$20**</u>

(b) <u>**$10 more**</u>

$$1 - \frac{1}{4} = \frac{3}{4}$$

Ethan had $\frac{3}{4}$ of his money left.

The ratio of the money Ethan had to the money Dakota had is:

Ethan : Dakota
5 : 7
or   15 : 21

Since $\frac{3}{4}$ (or 3 parts) of Ethan's money is 15 parts,

$$15 \div 3 = 5$$

$\frac{1}{4}$ of Ethan's money is 5 parts.

The ratio of the money Ethan had in the beginning to the money Dakota had is as follows:

Ethan : Dakota
15 + 5 : 21 − 5
20 : 16

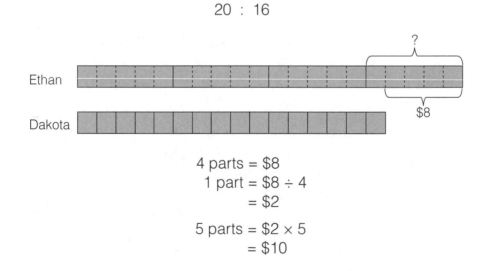

4 parts = $8
1 part = $8 ÷ 4
= $2

5 parts = $2 × 5
= $10

Ethan gave **$10** to Dakota.

Answer: _____**$10**_____

Solution to Question 55

Foreign stamps	
Local stamps	?
	80
	10

$$80 - 10 = 70$$

$$70 \div 5 = 14$$

$$
\begin{array}{r}
14 \\
5\overline{)70} \\
-5 \\
\hline
20 \\
-20 \\
\hline
0
\end{array}
$$

Each part is 14.

$$14 \times 2 = 28$$

$$28 + 10 = 38$$

He had **38** local stamps in the beginning.

Answer: **38 local stamps**

Since the fraction $\frac{3}{5}$ is used in the question, divide each part into 5 smaller parts in the illustration.

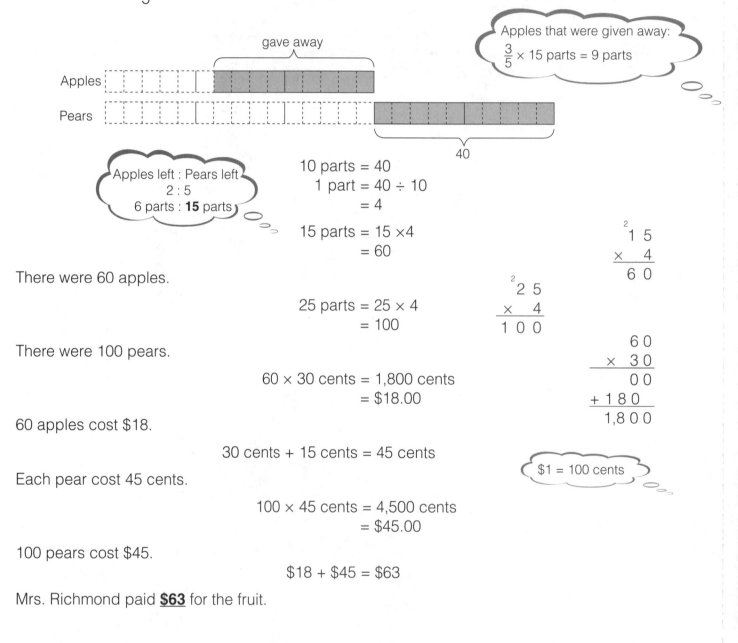

There were 60 apples.

There were 100 pears.

60 apples cost $18.

Each pear cost 45 cents.

100 pears cost $45.

Mrs. Richmond paid **$63** for the fruit.

Answer: **$63**

Solution to Question 57

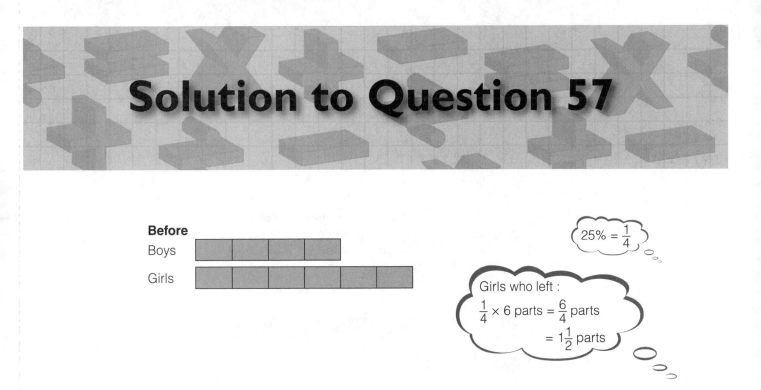

Before

Boys

Girls

25% = $\frac{1}{4}$

Girls who left :
$\frac{1}{4}$ × 6 parts = $\frac{6}{4}$ parts
= $1\frac{1}{2}$ parts

Since $1\frac{1}{2}$ parts of the number of girls had left, we can divide each part into 2 smaller parts.

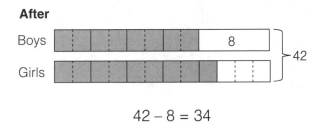

After

Boys — 8

Girls

42

$$42 - 8 = 34$$

$$17 \text{ parts} = 34$$
$$1 \text{ part} = 34 \div 17$$
$$= 2$$

Each part is 2.

$$20 \times 2 = 40$$

The total number of Art Club members at the beginning of the year was **40**.

Answer: **40 members**

Solution to Question 58

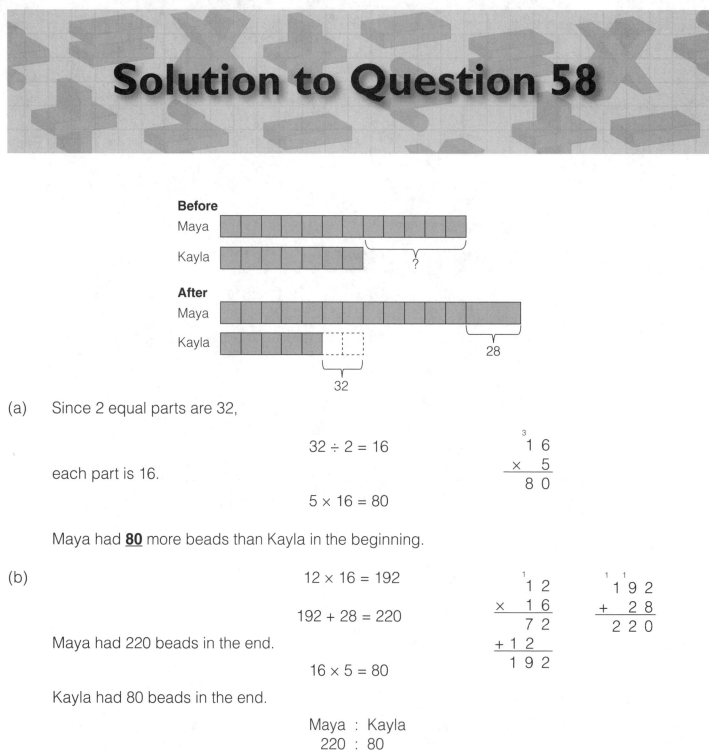

Before
Maya
Kayla
?

After
Maya
Kayla
32
28

(a) Since 2 equal parts are 32,

$$32 \div 2 = 16$$

each part is 16.

$$5 \times 16 = 80$$

$$\begin{array}{r} \overset{3}{1}\,6 \\ \times\quad 5 \\ \hline 8\,0 \end{array}$$

Maya had **80** more beads than Kayla in the beginning.

(b)

$$12 \times 16 = 192$$

$$192 + 28 = 220$$

Maya had 220 beads in the end.

$$16 \times 5 = 80$$

Kayla had 80 beads in the end.

$$\begin{array}{r} \overset{1}{1}\,2 \\ \times\quad 1\,6 \\ \hline 7\,2 \\ +\,1\,2\quad \\ \hline 1\,9\,2 \end{array}$$

$$\begin{array}{r} \overset{1}{1}\,\overset{1}{9}\,2 \\ +\quad 2\,8 \\ \hline 2\,2\,0 \end{array}$$

```
Maya : Kayla
 220 :  80
  22 :   8
  11 :   4
```

The new ratio of Maya's beads to Kayla's beads was **11 : 4**.

Answer: (a) **80 more beads**

    (b)   **11 : 4**

Before

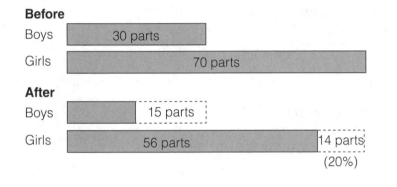

Boys | 30 parts

Girls | 70 parts

After

Boys | 15 parts

Girls | 56 parts | 14 parts
(20%)

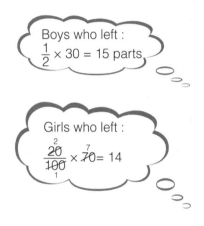

Boys who left :
$\frac{1}{2} \times 30 = 15$ parts

Girls who left :
$\frac{\overset{2}{20}}{\underset{1}{100}} \times \overset{7}{70} = 14$

15 parts + 14 parts = 29 parts

29 parts = 87 students
1 part = 87 ÷ 29
= 3 students

$$\begin{array}{r} 3 \\ 29\overline{)87} \\ -87 \\ \hline 0 \end{array}$$

70 parts = 70 × 3
= 210 students

210 girls were at the camp in the beginning.

Answer: ___**210 girls**___

$$30 \times \$1.50 = \$45$$

$$\$45 + \$10 = \$55$$

$$
\begin{array}{r}
\overset{1}{1}.5\,0 \\
\times \quad 3\,0 \\
\hline
0\,0\,0 \\
+\ 4\,5\,0 \\
\hline
4\,5.0\,0
\end{array}
$$

Ahmed earns $55 when he sells one carton of 30 video games.

$$\$450 \div \$55 = 8 \text{ R } 10$$

$$
\begin{array}{r}
8 \\
55\overline{)4\,5\,0} \\
-4\,4\,0 \\
\hline
1\,0
\end{array}
$$

He has to sell at least 8 cartons of 30 video games.

$$\$10 \div \$1.50 = 1000¢ \div 150¢$$
$$= 100 \div 15$$
$$= 6 \text{ R } 10$$

$1 = 100¢
$10 = 1,000¢

$$
\begin{array}{r}
6 \\
15\overline{)1\,0\,0} \\
-\ 9\,0 \\
\hline
1\,0
\end{array}
$$

He has to sell an additional 6 video games.

$$8 \text{ cartons} \times 30 = 240 \text{ video games}$$

$$240 + 6 = 246 \text{ video games}$$

The minimum number of video games he has to sell in order to earn $450 is **246**.

Answer : **246 video games**

Solution to Question 61

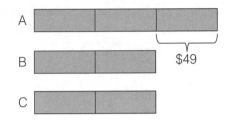

(a)

B's money : C's money

   2 : 2

   1 : 1

The ratio of B's money to C's money was **1 : 1**.

(b)

$$\$49 \times 2 = \$98$$

$$\begin{array}{r} {}^{1} \\ 4\ 9 \\ \times\ \ \ 2 \\ \hline 9\ 8 \end{array}$$

C received **$98**.

Answer: (a)   **1 : 1**

        (b)   **$98**

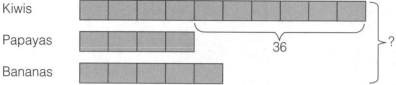

Since 6 equal parts are 36,

$$36 \div 6 = 6$$

each part is 6.

$$4 \text{ parts} + 5 \text{ parts} + 10 \text{ parts} = 19 \text{ parts}$$

$$19 \times 6 = 114$$

$$\begin{array}{r} {}^{5}1\,9 \\ \times 6 \\ \hline 1\,1\,4 \end{array}$$

There are **114** pieces of fruit in the basket.

Answer: **114 pieces of fruit**

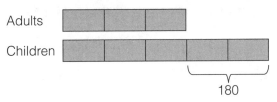

Since 2 equal parts are 180,

$$180 \div 2 = 90$$

each part is 90.

$$90 \times 5 = 450$$

There were 450 children.

Since 9 equal parts are 450,

$$450 \div 9 = 50$$

each part is 50.

$$5 \times 50 = 250$$

There were **250** more girls than boys at the party.

Answer: **250 more girls**

Solution to Question 64

C : Children
M : Men
W : Women

6 parts – 1 part = 5 parts

5 parts = 140

1 part = 140 ÷ 5
     = 28

$$\begin{array}{r} 28 \\ 5\overline{)140} \\ -10 \\ \hline 40 \\ -40 \\ \hline 0 \end{array}$$

There were 28 women at the funfair.

28 × 10 = 280

$$\begin{array}{r} 28 \\ \times\ 10 \\ \hline 00 \\ +28 \\ \hline 280 \end{array}$$

280 people went to the funfair.

Answer: **280 people**

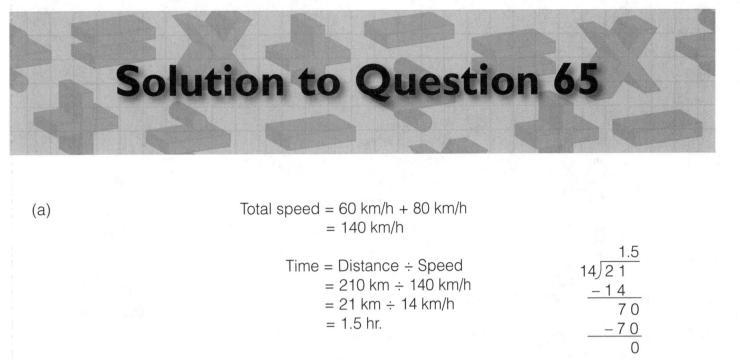

Solution to Question 65

(a)

$$\text{Total speed} = 60 \text{ km/h} + 80 \text{ km/h}$$
$$= 140 \text{ km/h}$$

$$\text{Time} = \text{Distance} \div \text{Speed}$$
$$= 210 \text{ km} \div 140 \text{ km/h}$$
$$= 21 \text{ km} \div 14 \text{ km/h}$$
$$= 1.5 \text{ hr.}$$

$$
\begin{array}{r}
1.5 \\
14\overline{)21} \\
-14 \\
\hline
70 \\
-70 \\
\hline
0 \\
\end{array}
$$

$$1.5 \text{ hr.} \times 60 \text{ min.} = 90 \text{ min.}$$

$$
\begin{array}{r}
60 \\
\times\ 1.5 \\
\hline
300 \\
+\ 60 \\
\hline
90.0 \\
\end{array}
$$

$$9\text{:}20 \text{ P.M.} + 90 \text{ min.}$$
$$= 9\text{:}20 \text{ P.M.} + 60 \text{ min.} + 30 \text{ min.}$$
$$= 10\text{:}20 \text{ P.M.} + 30 \text{ min.}$$
$$= 10\text{:}50 \text{ P.M.}$$

The car passed the bus at **10:50 P.M.**

(b)

$$\text{Distance} = \text{Speed} \times \text{Time}$$
$$= 80 \text{ km/h} \times 1.5 \text{ hr.}$$
$$= 120 \text{ km}$$

$$
\begin{array}{r}
80 \\
\times\ 1.5 \\
\hline
400 \\
+\ 80 \\
\hline
120.0 \\
\end{array}
$$

The car had traveled **120 km** when it passed the bus.

Answer: (a) __**10:50 P.M.**__

(b) __**120 km**__

(a)

$$\text{Distance} = \text{Speed} \times \text{Time}$$
$$\text{Speed} = \text{Distance} \div \text{Time}$$
$$= 40 \text{ km} \div \frac{1}{2} \text{ hr.} = 40 \times 2$$
$$= 80 \text{ km/h}$$

Stephen was driving at **80 km/h**.

(b) Time needed for Cole to catch up with Stephen
= Distance that Cole had to catch up ÷ difference in their speeds
= 40 km ÷ 30 km/h
$= \frac{4}{3}$ hr. $= 1\frac{1}{3}$ hr.

Cole needed $1\frac{1}{3}$ hours to catch up with Stephen.

Since Cole drove at a constant speed that was 30 km/h faster than Stephen,

$$80 \text{ km/h} + 30 \text{ km/h} = 110 \text{ km/h}$$

Cole drove at a speed of 110 km/h.

The distance that Cole drove in order to catch up with Stephen and arrive at the same time as Stephen is the distance between the 2 towns.

$$\text{Distance} = \text{Speed} \times \text{Time}$$
$$= 110 \text{ km/h} \times 1\frac{1}{3} \text{ hr.}$$
$$= 110 \times \frac{4}{3} = \frac{440}{3}$$
$$= 146\frac{2}{3} \text{ km}$$

```
      1 4 6
  3 ) 4 4 0
     - 3
      1 4
     - 1 2
        2 0
       - 1 8
          2
```

The distance between the 2 towns was **$146\frac{2}{3}$ km**.

Answer: (a) ___**80 km/h**___

(b) ___**$146\frac{2}{3}$ km**___

Solution to Question 67

1 part of rotten eggs = 6

3 parts of rotten eggs = 6 × 3 = 18

There were 18 rotten eggs.

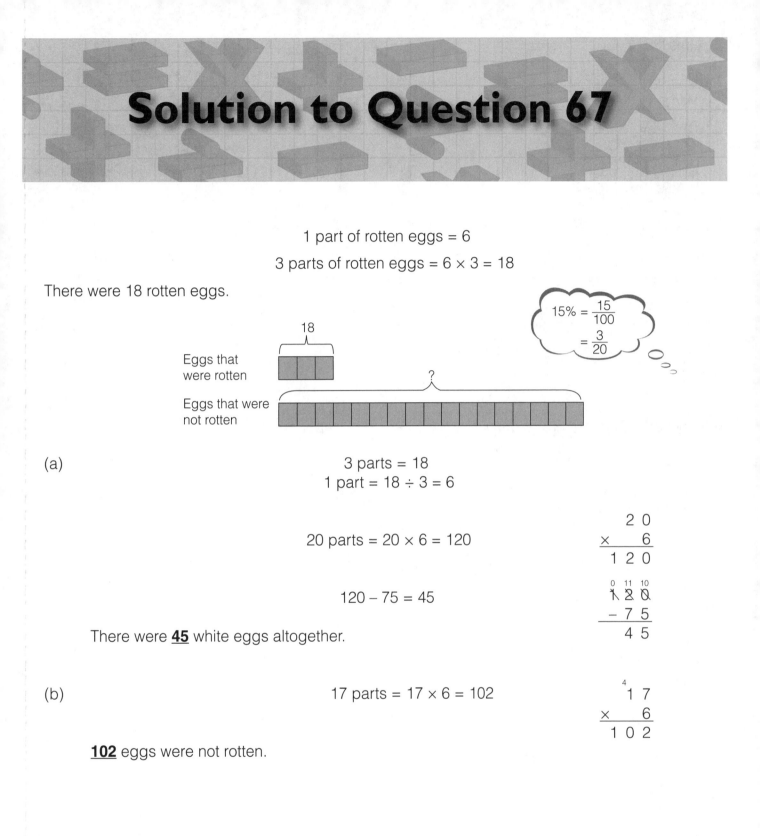

$15\% = \dfrac{15}{100}$
$= \dfrac{3}{20}$

18

Eggs that were rotten

?

Eggs that were not rotten

(a)

3 parts = 18

1 part = 18 ÷ 3 = 6

20 parts = 20 × 6 = 120

$$\begin{array}{r} 2\,0 \\ \times \quad 6 \\ \hline 1\,2\,0 \end{array}$$

120 − 75 = 45

$$\begin{array}{r} {}^{0}\!\!\!\!1\ {}^{11}\!2\ {}^{10}\!0 \\ -\quad 7\,5 \\ \hline 4\,5 \end{array}$$

There were **45** white eggs altogether.

(b)

17 parts = 17 × 6 = 102

$$\begin{array}{r} {}^{4}\ \\ 1\,7 \\ \times \quad 6 \\ \hline 1\,0\,2 \end{array}$$

102 eggs were not rotten.

Answer: (a) **45 white eggs**

(b) **102 eggs**

Solution to Question 68

$$\frac{3}{4} \times \overset{25}{\cancel{100}} = 75$$

$$\begin{array}{r} \overset{1}{2}\,5 \\ \times \quad 3 \\ \hline 7\,5 \end{array}$$

Brittany made 75 paper cranes.

$$\frac{9}{\underset{1}{\cancel{20}}} \times \overset{5}{\cancel{100}} = 45$$

Ava gave 45 paper cranes to Brittany.

$$75 + 45 = 120$$

Brittany had 120 paper cranes after Ava gave her some paper cranes.

$$\frac{1}{\underset{1}{\cancel{4}}} \times \overset{30}{\cancel{120}} = 30$$

Brittany gave 30 paper cranes to Ava.

$$100 - 45 = 55$$
$$55 + 30 = 85$$

Ava had 85 paper cranes in the end.

$$120 - 30 = 90$$

Brittany had 90 paper cranes in the end.

$$90 - 85 = 5$$

Brittany had **5** more paper cranes than Ava in the end.

Answer: **5 more paper cranes**

Solution to Question 69

Convert $2\frac{1}{2}$ into a mixed number,

$$2\frac{1}{2} = \frac{5}{2}$$

Before

Boy (Group A)

Girls (Group B)

$\left.\vphantom{\begin{array}{c}a\\b\end{array}}\right\}$ 490

Since 7 equal parts are 490,

$$490 \div 7 = 70$$

each part is 70.

$$70 \times 2 = 140$$

There were 140 boys in the beginning.

For every 4 boys, 32 more boys joined,

$$140 \div 4 = 35$$
$$35 \times 32 = 1,120$$

$$
\begin{array}{r}
3\,5 \\
4\overline{)1\,4\,0} \\
-1\,2 \\
\hline
2\,0 \\
-2\,0 \\
\hline
0
\end{array}
$$

$$
\begin{array}{r}
3\,5 \\
\times\ \ 3\,2 \\
\hline
7\,0 \\
+1\,0\,5\ \ \\
\hline
1,1\,2\,0
\end{array}
$$

1,120 more boys joined the group.

$$1,120 + 140 = 1,260$$

There were 1,260 boys in the end.

$$\frac{1}{3} \times 1,260 = 420$$

There were 420 girls in the end.

$$
\begin{array}{r}
4\,2\,0 \\
3\overline{)1,2\,6\,0} \\
-1\,2\ \ \ \ \\
\hline
6\ \ \\
-6\ \ \\
\hline
0 \\
-0 \\
\hline
0
\end{array}
$$

$$70 \times 5 = 350$$
$$420 - 350 = 70$$

70 more girls joined the group.

$$\frac{\text{Girls who joined Group B}}{\text{Boys who joined Group A}} = \frac{7}{1,120} = \frac{7}{112} = \frac{1}{16}$$

The fraction is $\frac{1}{16}$.

Answer: $\dfrac{1}{16}$

$$\$825 \times 80\% = \$825 \times \frac{80}{100}$$
$$= \$825 \times \frac{4}{5}$$
$$= \$660$$

$$\begin{array}{r} {}^{2}1\,{}^{2}6\,5 \\ \times \qquad 4 \\ \hline 6\,6\,0 \end{array}$$

The computer cost $660.

12%	88%

| Car repairs | Food | | | |

$1,320 + $660

$25\% = \frac{1}{4}$

3 parts = $1,320 + $660
= $1,980

$$\begin{array}{r} 1,3\,2\,0 \\ +\quad 6\,6\,0 \\ \hline 1,9\,8\,0 \end{array}$$

1 part = $1,980 ÷ 3
= $660

$$\begin{array}{r} 660 \\ 3\overline{)1,980} \\ -18 \\ \hline 18 \\ -18 \\ \hline 0 \\ -0 \\ \hline 0 \end{array}$$

4 parts = $660 × 4
= $2,640

$$\begin{array}{r} {}^{2}6\,6\,0 \\ \times \qquad 4 \\ \hline 2,6\,4\,0 \end{array}$$

The remaining 88% of the money was $2,640.

88% → $2,640
1% → $2,640 ÷ 88
= $30
100% → 100 × $30
= $3,000

$$\begin{array}{r} 30 \\ 88\overline{)2,640} \\ -264 \\ \hline 0 \\ -0 \\ \hline 0 \end{array}$$

Nate had **$3,000** in the beginning.

Answer: ___**$3,000**___

Notes

Notes

Notes

Notes

Notes

Notes

Notes

Notes